The Best of Bishop

MORRIS BISHOP

The Best of Bishop

Light Verse from
The New Yorker and Elsewhere

MORRIS BISHOP

EDITED AND WITH AN INTRODUCTION BY
Charlotte Putnam Reppert

FOREWORD BY
David McCord

DRAWINGS BY
Alison Mason Kingsbury
AND Richard Taylor

Cornell University Press

ITHACA AND LONDON

First published 1980 by Cornell University Press.
Published in the United Kingdom by Cornell University Press Ltd., 2-4 Brook Street, London W1Y 1AA.

The poems on pages 31-33, 35, 40, 42, 45, 50-51, 57, 64, 69-71, 73, 77, 81, 84-85, 90-91, 93, 102-105, 107-108, 114-18, 120-24, 128-32, 136, 138, 141-43, 146-48, 151, 154-55, 158-60, 162-65, 168, 170, 171, 209, 211, 213, 215, 219 and 221 originally appeared in *The New Yorker* and are published here by arrangement with Alison Mason Kingsbury Bishop.

The poems on pages 30, 34, 36-39, 41, 43, 46-49, 52-56, 58-63, 65-68, 72, 75-76, 78-79, 83, 86-88, 95-98, 100-101, 106, 109, 113, 119, 125-26, 135, 139-40, 149-50, 152, 157, 161, 171, and 177-205 are reprinted by permission of G. P. Putnam's Sons from *Spilt Milk* by Morris Bishop. Copyright 1942, renewed © copyright 1969 by Morris Bishop.

The poems on pages 25, 94, 133-34, 144-45, 153, and 169 are reprinted from *The Saturday Evening Post,* © 1926, 1928, 1930, 1931, 1932, The Curtis Publishing Company.

"To Lands of Wonder" is copyright © 1960 by The New York Times Company. Reprinted by permission.

Drawings on pages 32-33 by Rea Irvin are copyright © 1946, 1974 The New Yorker Magazine, Inc.

Lines in the Foreword from "The Midnight Skaters," by Edmund Blunden, are reproduced from *Poems of Many Years,* by permission of A. D. Peters & Co. Ltd. "Pediatric Reflection," by Ogden Nash, from *Verses from 1929 On,* copyright 1931 by Ogden Nash, is quoted by permission of Little, Brown & Co., and Curtis Brown, Ltd.

International Standard Book Number 0-8014-1310-9
Library of Congress Catalog Card Number 80-66902
Printed in the United States of America
Librarians: Library of Congress cataloging information appears on the last page of the book.

Foreword

Here in verse unrivalled not only in its day but of its kind is the best of Morris Bishop. And the best of Morris Bishop, I quickly add, arranged in easy potlatch splendor for those fortunate readers whose love of wit and craftsmanship in both prose and verse has turned them more than once to any such as Horace, Herrick, Peacock, Praed, Lear, Carroll, Calverley, Gilbert, Beerbohm, Sarah Orne Jewett, Chesterton, James Stephens, Don Marquis, Joyce, Perelman, Thurber, Clarence Day, Nabokov, Auden, and MacNeice.

Now, that fine word *potlatch* was not drummed up along the Mohawk. Pure northwest Chinook it is (from Nootka): meaning a ceremonial feast "at the end of which the host gives valuable material goods to his guests." Well, all these verses—most of them taken from the old *New Yorker* of Harold Ross—are, at this anxious goldbrick moment, valuable material goods available in a world where laughter has turned hollow because we suffer from a shifty new pyemia: apprehension in the blood. It seems to me as sad as it is strange in a very strange sad way not to believe in a large and instant audience for this brilliant collection, so witty and so wide in range and technique that no Book-of-the-Month Club today will dare to snap it up. What matter that most of it speaks here out of context from the pages of a magazine between the two World Wars when wits were supple, active, fresh, and in good supply? You know all their names: White, Thurber, Benchley, Sullivan, Parker, Woollcott, Nash, McGinley, and two or three others. Look! The films of Chaplin, Buster Keaton, and W. C. Fields are still popular, though Disney, Magoo, and the short classic reels of Robert Benchley drift, alas, in faint penumbral shadow. Great cartoonists of the Ross era (Arno and Hokinson) continue in book form; Saul Steinberg, the "lean" George Price, and the "fat" Charles Addams draw as well and about as often as ever.

But what we call light verse? It has vanished almost completely from such as *The New Yorker, Harper's, Atlantic, Saturday Review.* Nash and McGinley persist in their books; Sissman as well. Richard Wilbur—see his *Opposites*—John Frederick Nims, Robert Fitzgerald, George Starbuck, Howard Moss, and William Jay Smith can, as could Auden, so easily cross south into the lighter country when they care to. John Ciardi is frequently there in his remarkable verse for children. But from the twenties on down into the fifties there was Morris Bishop, the one true poet at heart who moved with almost elfin grace amid, yet superior to, the difficulties of an art traditionally chained and fettered by strict rhyme and meter. He moved with grace in the way the classicist will slipper through the ablatives, genders, gerunds, deponents, inversions and flexible word order to the core of Horace, Catullus, and Martial; moving to lend his wit and tremendous satiric talent to the writing of what we call light verse.

Consider this field into which he entered. There are not many poets, English or American, whom we respect *solely* for the light verse which they have written. But few will deny that there is genuine quality in the cheerful work of Calverley, Praed, Lear, Carroll (essentially the parodist), Gilbert, Don Marquis, Nabokov, John Updike; not overlooking in the lighter vein a number of poems by Eliot, Edith Sitwell, Auden, Ivor Richards, MacNeice, Roethke, Henry Reed, Stevie Smith, Nemerov, and Wilbur—all of them poets in the serious galaxy. Surely Walter de la Mare had his moments of lightness not alone in *Peacock Pie* but in the whole long lyric stretch of his poetic life. Or take Edmund Blunden whose reputation as a poet does not measure up to his splendid performance. What about that acrobatic poem called "The Midnight Skaters"—poetry with a scary premise, yet bright at its best and airiest? It begins in sheer delight:

> The hop-poles stand in cones,
> The icy pond lurks under,
> The pole-tops steeple to the thrones

> Of stars, sound gulfs of wonder;
> But not the tallest there, 'tis said,
> Could fathom to this pond's black bed.

Two more stanzas, and the poem ends with these words, nimble as the very thought of blades on dangerous ice:

> Dance on this ball-floor thin and wan,
> Use him as though you love him;
> Court him, elude him, reel and pass,
> And let him hate you through the glass.

This poem by a very serious poet suggests one important fact about the so-called art of light verse: it must be brief and it must have absolutely no weakness in it. Like an egg, it is either good or bad—no in between. In the writing of it there is no substitute for discipline, endless drill, and infinite patience. The devious, the labyrinthine form is fatal to wit, fatal to humor. Brevity *dictates* perfection. In a long serious poem there is space for the inevitable wayward passage, for the outright solecism:

> With nectar pure his oozy locks he laves

doesn't *sound* like Milton at his peerless best; but there it is in *Lycidas*. And what of that joggy trackmeet line in *Kubla Khan* anticipating a slang word undreamed of by Coleridge:

> As if the earth in fast thick pants were breathing.

George Saintsbury, generous but no easy-going critic, said this of light verse: "A low kind of art? That does not seem a necessary subject of discussion. The point is that it is the very highest kind of its own art; and that is all we have to do with. An easy kind of art? Go thou and do likewise." So in fact I hold with Archibald MacLeish who wrote the sensitive and analeptic introduction to the selected poems of Ogden Nash: *I Wouldn't Have Missed It* (Little, Brown, 1975). MacLeish came straight to the point: Light verse? "One objection to the term: it is inaccurate. The other is the implication. 'Light Verse' carries a demeaning connotation. It implies that the art of poetry has its Macy's basement where a kind of second-rate excellence is the criterion. And this, of course, is an affront to poetry. There is only one kind of poetry: poetry. The art has no departments."

So now, in isolating a few scattered lines from among Morris Bishop's poems in this book, I pay them no casual honor in silhouetting them against some fragments from the poetry of established poets, whose principal work, by no means of a lighter sort, you find in the latest *Oxford Book of Verse* or other respectable places. Bishop, remember, was a first-class scholar and linguist: a polymath. He spoke flawless French. He could speak Latin as can few scholars of my acquaintance. Of course Bishop knew both Spanish and Italian and who can say what else as well. And yet his verse is never crippled by abstruse or unfamiliar words. He gave to the commonplace the dignity of simple speech arranged with the balance and insight only the true poet can miraculously manage.

When Nabokov in the tiniest of essays speaks of some gigantic black pipes lying in single file at the outer edge of a Berlin sidewalk, he is delighted one morning to observe an even strip of fresh snow along the upper side of each pipe, and the large word "Otto" which someone had written with one finger on one of them. He thought "how beautifully that name, with its two soft o's flanking the pair of gentle consonants, suited the silent layer of snow upon that pipe with its two orifices and its tacit tunnel." You will note again the same "two gentle consonants" which compress the brief word "tacit" into itself. Such is the tidy mind of the tidy poet at his task. It is what Morris Bishop would have observed and thought; and the likely point he would have made out of the observation. The poet *sees* with his ear. Nabokov *heard* what he saw.

Now one of the best and most memorable of Morris Bishop's poems is "Mournful Numbers" which, as his constant readers will admit, endures as an example of firmly controlled pure nostalgia. More enduring, perhaps, for those of us of the pre-dialling era; and yet so honest in teenage point of view that it survives all date lines. It begins:

> Where in the attic the dust encumbers
> Days that are gone,
> I found a paper with telephone numbers
> Scribbled thereon.

Repeat that opening line slowly to yourself. How could one fit together seven better chosen words to release this particular fragment of poetry? Observe that with "encumbers" you have a feminine ending, and rightly guess the poem's nostalgia; and *then* note how exquisitely the first line *ends* with the updraft of "encumbers" and yet carries over smoothly to the solidity of "Days." It is not just the flawless masonry of that first line which now enchants the reader but the following choice of "Days" for what John Ciardi would call the fulcrum word. Substitute "Time" or any other possible word and the magic has evaporated. Indeed, magic is what I am talking about. Ear told the poet what to write, just as Ralph Hodgson's ear dictated the correct solution for a line in "The Song of Honour" which a lesser poet would not have resolved. At one point in this poem (which should outlast everything else Ralph Hodgson ever wrote) we come upon the line

> Among the plums and apple trees

and may wonder how it is that the plums deserve mention when the apples do not. Furthermore, the grammar disturbs with "plums trees." But if the poet had written the correct noun-adjective "plum" the reader would find that this (when read aloud) throws the "d" of "and" against the "a" of "apple," turning it into "dapple." The poet's ear again! Forget about grammar: The plural "plums" pulls the "a" of "and" in toward it and releases the "d" so that

> Among the plums and apple trees

is (to me at least) a musical and memorable line enchanting as Bishop's

> Where in the attic the dust encumbers. . . .

Watch for many such subleties in the pages ahead of you. But right now let me equate, not alone in terms of charm but in terms of time, this opening stanza from "Mournful numbers" with three lines of de la Mare at his best:

> Oh no man knows
> Through what wild centuries
> Roves back the rose.

Not a comparison of *light verse* to poetry; but of *poetry* to poetry.

I seem to remember, though I haven't looked it up for fear I may be wrong, that Helen Waddell concludes her study of the Wandering Scholars with that same quotation from the author of *Peacock Pie*. I think it would have pleased Morris that I choose to say this, for is there not a kind of Horatian reversal in "roves back the rose"?

For sixty years the opening lines of Thomas Love Peacock's "The War Song of Dinas Vwar" have crossed and recrossed my mind. An accepted poem by the Oxford and many other editors, it is truly on the bloody light side; and yet it is poetry.

> The mountain sheep are sweeter,
> But the valley sheep are fatter;
> We therefor deemed it meeter
> To carry off the latter.

Well, with what else in spirit and for the sheer pleasure of equating two poets blest with technical skill and that perfect ear which Eliot praised in Tennyson would you compare this quotation? You would compare it with Bishop's "We Have Been Here Before." Take the opening two lines of any stanza in this poem out of context; look at the fragment of Peacock above; then read (I trust with similar delight):

> "I have been here before," I asserted,
> In a nook on a neck of the Nile.

Even in verses which require some quoted material to justify his satiric intention, Bishop sets his course, choosing his words—and using them—with elegance. Take, for example, the closing stanza in "A Salute to the Modern Language Association, Convening in the Hotel Pennsylvania":

> May your influence quell, like a panacea,
> A business assembly's financial fevers,
> With the faint, sweet memory of "Observaciones sobre
> la aspiración de H en Andalucía,"
> And "The Stimmsprung (Voice Leap) of Sievers."

Bishop is never concerned with *creating* nonsense words as were with supreme success, for example, Edward Lear, Lewis Carroll, James Joyce. This was all no go with Eliot, who greatly admired Lear; nor was it any go with Ogden Nash beyond his extraordinary skill with—and his stranglehold on—warping and telescoping ordinary words to fit his rhyme control, viz.:

> Many an infant that screams like a calliope
> Could be soothed by a little attention to its diope.

But when Morris Bishop needed to create some nonsense words for his masterpiece of devastating satire on baby-talk,* "A Tonversation with Baby," he was a Lear reborn. I think you will agree that the old Nonsense Master's "Sparry in the pilderpips" or "The Yongy-Bongy Bo" in no way surpasses this joyous Bishop couplet aimed at the lively contents of a baby carriage:

> O tweety goo swummy doodle,
> O yummy yum.

But better and surely more subtle than a private syllabus of even excellent nonsense words in declaration of a nonsense poem are a couple of seamless quatrains producing the *effect* of nonsense simply by an unexpected grouping of ordinary words, or by the threading of a string of them like beads in some unusual way. Bishop was adept at this sort of thing: "The Anatomy

---

*The reader may reflect (as most likely did Morris Bishop) on Brother Egidio's epigram: "The Bible is God talking baby-talk."

of Humor," "Fragment from 'The Maladjusted: A Tragedy,'"
"The Adventures of Id," "Not Unmindful of the Negative as I
Am Not." Tops of them all in this category is

The Naughty Preposition

> I lately lost a preposition;
>   It hid, I thought, beneath my chair.
> And angrily I cried: "Perdition!
>   Up from out of in under there!"
>
> Correctness is my vade mecum,
>   And straggling phrases I abhor;
> And yet I wondered: "What should he come
>   Up from out of in under for?"

Many poets—many very good poets—commit the dismaying
error of assuming that a certain word or pair of words, or even a
complete line, will read with the inflection the writer intended.
They forget that "can not," for example, may in reality be "*can*
not" or "can *not*"; "he come" may be either "*he* come" or simply a
fairly level "he come" with just the faintest of accent on "come."
What does Bishop do with this second combination? Why, his
controlling rhyme words are in Latin: "vade mecum," which
admits of but one pronunciation of "*he* come." Consequently no
intelligent reader will stumble over that third line. And thinking
of foolproof control, do not overlook at the close of this volume
the most homogeneous flock of limericks ever to take wing in the
English language: not one line in the total flight which doesn't
scan as well as make its point.

> There's a vaporish maiden in Harrison
> Who longed for the love of a Saracen.
>   But she had to confine her
>   Intent to a Shriner,
> Who suffers, I fear, by comparison.

Bishop, a traveller abroad, surely loved his food. His gas-
tronomic sonnet-satire concerning the communal gloom of the

grapefruit and dried chicken circuit is a small classic in banquet isolation. What poet dead or alive could outdo these opening lines found scribbled on the back of a menu?

> In the wide banquet dreadfully alone
> I watch the jaws that swing upon their hinges,
> The upward chump-chump-chumping that impinges
> The golden inlay on the enamelled bone. . . .

In his own words which he does not use to describe these or any other lines he ever wrote, they give to me "a piercing pleasure." A piercing pleasure? I would know at a glance that Morris Bishop put that adjective and that noun together. And if you should read "And We in Dreams Behold the Hebrides," will you ever forget the opening?

> Divine Nostalgia! Admirable boon,
> Turning the homing heart to yesteryear. . . .

I doubt it.

We may sometimes suspect writers of writing their own dustjackets. Bishop once wrote one for his book called *A Bowl of Bishop.* I quote the final paragraphs:

> Mr. Bishop's thought is sometimes baffling, hermetic, obscure. It tends, indeed, toward the annihilation of all thought. His *style* is often characterized as brittle, salty, and astringent, like a pretzel. In order to express his difficult philosophy, he has been obliged to use *words.* Many of these are remarkable, full of shadings, nuances, and vowel-colors. The author is a partisan of pure *form.* One will note particularly his sensitive treatment of diphthongs.
>
> Mr. Bishop's *influence* has been negligible.

Now it would not seem proper to close this overlong prelude to the gospel of Bishop without dipping into his one jewel of biography, *St. Francis of Assisi.* He relates how as a very young man this future saint discovered a tiny chapel in sorry disrepair. He restored it, and it came to be called (in translation) Little Portion or Small Holding. In the busy life of a classical scholar,

Foreword

Morris Bishop just as surely created his own Little Portion or Small Holding. Perhaps like St. Francis—more endearingly, Il Poverello—Morris deliberately chose that intimate vein of poetry which would delight. And surely we can do with all the St. Francis that is in him, if not in us! Well, according to his biographer, St. Francis himself was unpredictable in certain notions. Morris Bishop was *always* unpredictable in his choice of subjects when it came to verse. Which is why I take it for truth that one day in Ithaca he set out to buy a loaf of bread—a truly Franciscan mission—and returned wearing a new beret and driving a new white Jaguar.

DAVID McCORD

Boston, Massachusetts

14

Contents

Contents

Contents

Contents

Introduction

Morris Gilbert Bishop took wry amusement in the fact that he was born in an institution for the insane. His father, a Canadian physician named Edwin R. Bishop, was a member of the staff of Willard State Hospital in upstate New York at the time of his son's birth on April 15, 1893. On the death of his mother two years later, Morris and his three-year-old brother Edwin were sent to his Canadian grandparents in Brantford, Ontario. At the ages of eight and nine they were returned to Dr. Bishop, who by then had remarried and was practicing medicine in Geneva, New York. Within three years, tuberculosis had claimed the lives of both the stepmother and Dr. Bishop, and the boys were sent to the American side of the family in Yonkers, New York, where they lived until after graduation from college.

Entering Cornell on a scholarship in 1910, Morris Bishop achieved an enviable undergraduate record for writing, won a Phi Beta Kappa key and the Morrison Poetry Prize along with his B.A. in 1913, and attained the M.A. in 1914, his official Cornell class.

After a year selling textbooks in Boston and San Francisco for Ginn and Company, he joined a cavalry troop in order to ride, an activity that soon lost its glamour when he found himself on the Mexican border with Pershing, chasing full tilt after Pancho Villa. It was this little-known episode in his life that gave him a permanent dislike of horses ("stupid animals!").

During World War I Bishop served as liaison officer in the U.S. Infantry, earning his first lieutenant's commission.

A brief and disillusioning stint in a New York advertising agency after the Armistice was happily terminated by his acceptance of an instructorship at Cornell ("the most sensible thing I ever did"), where he became Romance languages professor until his alleged retirement in 1960.

With occasional interruptions for various long stays abroad, including overseas service for two years during World War II, when he did civilian liaison work, broadcasting, and other jobs, he remained on the Ithaca campus "happily teaching, reading and writing," until his death of a heart attack on November 20, 1973. He is survived by his widow, the artist Alison Mason Kingsbury, whom he married in 1927, and one daughter, Alison Bishop Jolly, who with her husband and four children resides in England.

Bishop's scholarly bent did not keep him from active involvement in university affairs. "As I look back," writes Mrs. Bishop, "I think that the most furiously active part of Morris's life came after his retirement." He was much sought after as a speaker on various public occasions; he inspired many undergraduates in his role as savant and bon vivant in Book and Bowl, a literary and social club for faculty and students; he continued to work actively in learned societies such as the Modern Language Association, of which he was president in 1964; and he will long be remembered by Cornellians everywhere for the celebrated incident of the Wielding of the Mace at commencement ceremonies in 1970, at the time of Dale Corson's formal investiture as president. To quote Editor John Marcham, in *Cornell Alumni News*, January 1974:

> A former student returned to Ithaca to make a public witness at Commencement that year . . . rushed the stage . . . [and] headed for the microphone on the lectern. Bishop, standing nearby, swung the fourteen-pound silver and gold mace from his shoulder and jabbed it smartly into [the intruder's] ribs in an effort to divert him. . . . [He] was soon dragged off by campus police, but not before news writers had been provided with a colorful story of how a 77-year-old professor in full academic regalia had used a historic symbol of authority to attack a modern day infidel.

Frequently during the past months devoted to collecting and editing the materials for *The Best of Bishop*, I have found myself in imaginary conversation with Professor Bishop explaining how and why this book happened. The bare facts are simple: one of his French literature students, whose face and name he would not even recognize, returning to Cornell forty years after graduation, tries to buy a copy of Bishop in the Campus Store, learns to her indignation that all his books of poems are out of print, starts agitating for somebody to do something about correcting this lamentable state of affairs, and to her surprise ends up doing it herself.

This book is the outcome of my long campaign to restore Morris Bishop to print.

So much for "how." I had three reasons "why."

Morris Bishop's own words supply part of the answer. In a midcareer autobiographical sketch for *Twentieth Century Authors* he surveyed his achievement with typical candor:

> In college and afterward I wrote a lot of poetry, some of which was published, even reaching the anthologies. But I had to recognize that I had nothing to say which had not been better said by others. The lyric urge of youth dwindled and died, leaving behind a certain amount of technique, which would serve, I discovered, for light verse. When, sadly wounded, I abandoned the business battle, I found that I could sell my little witticisms in verse and prose. So for thirty years I have contributed to the old *Life,* the *Saturday Evening Post,* and the *New Yorker.* Two* volumes of my light verse have appeared, and maybe there will be another.

"Maybe there will be another." Hardly a commitment to the public: just a semi-promise to himself, made by a scholar deeply involved in the demands of an academic career of teaching, writing, and speaking—a man confident that the wellsprings of his humorous inspiration would continue to flow, spilling out week after week in the pages of his favorite magazines a profusion of poems that would eventually be bottled like sparkling wine in a fourth book of verse.

But it was not to happen during his lifetime. In the last ten years of his life Bishop published almost exclusively in prose. The poems for *The New Yorker* ceased after 1960, those for

---

*Actually there had already been three: *Paramount Poems* (Minton, Balch, 1929) was later incorporated into *Spilt Milk* (G. P. Putnam's, 1943), which was followed by *A Bowl of Bishop* (Dial, 1954).

Saturday Review after 1964. In their place he wove a rich tapestry of varied short prose articles exploring, as he put it, "the delightful diversities of human behavior" as revealed in such personalities as Dante, Petrarch, Machiavelli, La Rochefoucauld, Louis-Philippe, and Nabokov, and in such eclectic subjects as the Oneida Community, the Norman Conquest, the perfect university, literary research, diction and usage, and the "Mississippi Bubble" real estate promotion of 1720.

During this period Bishop also published an impressive number of full-length works, among them his superlative *History of Cornell,* two books about Petrarch, one about Pascal, a life of St. Francis of Assisi, four books of stories from the classical, medieval, Renaissance, and romantic periods, and a collection called *The Exotics,* vignettes of twenty-one men and women whose unique personalities and remarkable characters appealed to what E. B. White (Cornell 1921) termed Professor Bishop's "infinite zest for life."

These literary accomplishments by a man in his seventies demonstrate the amazing enthusiasm and energy both as scholar and as campus figure that elicited from his classmate, humorist Frank Sullivan, the awed compliment, "I am forced to the conclusion that in addition to his talent he has been privately blessed with a twenty-eight hour day. Nothing else accounts for the remarkable body of work this versatile and gifted man has accomplished."

So it pleases me to think that in rescuing his shrewdest, shortest, funniest pieces from oblivion I am doing only what Morris Bishop would have done himself if he had found the time. That is my first reason.

My second is purely selfish. I wanted these poems for sanity's sake—not only those in *Spilt Milk* and *A Bowl of Bishop* (after all, those volumes are available in libraries if not in book stores) but also some I dimly recalled having snipped from periodicals but subsequently lost. Those who, like me, have been tormented by a choice but imperfectly recalled Bishop poem that refused either to emerge clearly or to fade completely from memory now stand a good chance of finding easement. This collection includes a sampling of the "little witticisms" that brightened the pages of magazines over a period of forty years but remained uncollected until now.

The third reason for this book's appearance lies, quite simply, in the fun of it. Light verse, Morris Bishop wrote, "observes truth with laughter, not with tears."* For decades his poems did just that, wryly revealing our quirks and foibles and reminding us to stop taking ourselves so seriously. And our laughter springs only in part from what he says; it's—well, let him have the floor again in this triolet from *The Saturday Evening Post,* back in April 1932:

> It wasn't so much what he said
> As the way that he said it;
> I laugh till I'm pretty near dead!
> Though it wasn't so much what he said.
> As I giggle my friends have fled,
> For they find it so hard to credit
> That it wasn't so much what he said
> As the way he said it!

The way Morris said it certainly accounts for the delight these poems bring to their intended audience, the "average educated man" he refers to in his essay "On Light Verse." Yet, however ingenious the rhyme, intricate the meter, or preposterous the idea, reason eventually prevails. I know of no better antidote for pomposity, sentimentality, and phony intellectualism than a frequent sampling of these verses, so meticulously crafted and so devastating in their honesty.

It is my hope and belief that those who knew him and those who never had that privilege will welcome Morris Bishop back into a world that needs all the truth and all the laughter it can get.

Selection of the poems for this volume was indeed difficult. The editor apologizes to outraged Bishop fans for the inevitable omission of special favorites.

*In "On Light Verse," which appeared as an introduction to *A Bowl of Bishop,* and was also published in *Harper's Magazine* in March 1954.

The poems, representing some forty years of productivity, have been taken out of chronological order and rearranged to assure the maximum display of their variety and originality.

I wish to thank David McCord, poet, essayist, and editor, for his support and encouragement in the adventure of editing this book. Mr. McCord's long friendship with Morris Bishop plus his own widely acclaimed skill in light-versifying (if he will pardon the term) led him to propose this same undertaking to Cornell University Press several years ago, but his many other commitments pressured him to turn the job over to me. I am grateful for his trust, his experience, and his invaluable suggestions in the final preparation of the manuscript.

Alison Mason Kingsbury (Mrs. Morris Bishop), whose charming illustrations enhance so many of these pages, has been an unfailing source of information, encouragement, and enthusiasm. Her friendship is one of the happiest fringe benefits of the entire project.

To John Marcham, editor of *Cornell Alumni News*, my thanks for his interest in the book and for permitting me to quote from his moving tribute to Morris Bishop in the January 1974 issue.

Thanks also to Mrs. John Hermansader, the former Mrs. Richard Taylor, for permission to use the sketches by her late husband, without which Bishop's limericks would be less wickedly funny.

Finally, thanks to my husband, Charles Miller Reppert, Cornell '34, who never dreamed that his undergraduate association with Professor Bishop in Book and Bowl would lead to the shared commitment that has brought these poems back into print.

CHARLOTTE PUTNAM REPPERT

Stratford, Connecticut

The Best of Bishop

Dear Reader

'Twas long ago, in Boston, Mass., I knew a wise old person.
(He was an advertising man named Edward K. McPherson.)
Esthetic problems he'd resolve in words I've not forgotten.
"It's all a question of taste," he'd say, "and your taste
                is rotten."

How often I have found myself disputing with the thinkers
If works of art are good or bad or absolutely stinkers!
And very often I'd get out of arguments I'd got in;
"It's all a question of taste," I'd say, "and your taste
                is rotten."

Many a man has read my rhymes and did not like a word of 'em;
And very many more there be who never even heard of 'em.
I do not mind if you should find these poems misbegotten;
"It's all a question of taste," I'd say, "and your taste
                is rotten."

—MORRIS BISHOP

Striking the Keynote

We are the generation
   That is too early wise;
We look upon creation
   With clear, untroubled eyes.
We see the world's illusion,
   We know that we must bear
Deep in our minds, confusion,
   Deep in our hearts, despair.

Our dreary fathers bound us
   Apprentices to pain;
The great machines impound us,
   Freedom and joy are vain;
No light, and no interstice
   In the blind trackless wood.
(What makes me feel the worst is
   I'm feeling pretty good.)

And sorrow's shafts in plenty
   Within us mortify;
The lads of one-and-twenty
   In sixty years must die.
Agony is our master!
   We must surrender to
Despair, death, doom, disaster!
   Toodle-y-oodle-y-oo!

The Anatomy of Humor

"What is funny?" you ask, my child,
  Crinkling your bright blue eye.
"Ah, that is a curious question indeed,"
  Musing, I make reply.

"Contusions are funny, not open wounds;
  And automobiles that go
Crash into trees by the highway-side;
  Industrial accidents, no.

"The habit of drink is a hundred per cent,
  But drug addiction is nil;
A nervous breakdown will get no laughs;
  Insanity surely will.

"Humor, aloof from the cigarette,
  Inhabits the droll cigar;
The middle-aged are not very funny;
  The young and the old, they are.

"So the funniest thing in the world should be
  A grandsire, drunk, insane,
Maimed in a motor-accident,
  And enduring moderate pain.

"But why do you scream and yell, my child?
  Here comes your mother, my honey,
To comfort you and to lecture me
  For trying, she'll say, to be funny."

Bard, Brush and Comb

In Classic times (which saucy youths rebuke),
Poesy wore the elegant peruke.
Decorum tamed the poet's boist'rous rhyme,
As chaste Decorum rear'd the wig sublime.
The tangled trope—or curl—would find no shrift
From such a minstrel as the Good Dean Swift.

The Romantics came down like a wolf on the fold,
And their poems were gleaming with purple and gold,
And the blustering wind of the heterodox
Bedevilled their verse and dishevelled their locks.

And after many a season
　　The stoic bards arrive;
Against the world's unreason
　　They are too proud to strive.

They pace the old quadrangle
　　In academic gown,
To see the lads a-dangle,
　　To watch the lasses drown.

Though they be canker-hearted,
　　They hide the inward smart;
Their hair is neatly parted
　　If they have hair to part.

So time came riding on its cracked
Bicycle, and undid the Present, mal-
　　odorous package. The young
　　Quake with social awareness,

Write tousled, rumpled, tangled lines
(O so artfully, so cunningly tousled!)
　　Under perplexed hair, perplexed
　　Whether they ought or whether they auden.

Some Think It's Dumb

Airmen do somersaults
   Far overhead;
Submarines grovel
   On the sea's bed;
Out of the atmosphere
   Far voices come;
Some think it's wonderful,
   Some think it's dumb.

Our little universe
   Charges through space,
Dodging the others
   All over the place;
Life began cell-wise
   In primeval scum;
Some think it's marvellous,
   Some think it's dumb.

Commodore Peary
   Went into the north;
Moses hit rocks
   And water came forth;
Socrates planned
   The Republic to come;
Some were delighted,
   But some thought it dumb.

The world is so wonderful,
   Life is so queer,
Let's be excited
   As long as we're here.
Of my philosophy
   That is the sum.
I think it's pretty good;
   Some think it's dumb.

The Naughty Preposition

I lately lost a preposition;
It hid, I thought, beneath my chair.
And angrily I cried: "Perdition!
Up from out of in under there!"

Correctness is my vade mecum,
And straggling phrases I abhor;
And yet I wondered: "What should he come
Up from out of in under for?"

K. O. Cook of Keokuk

K. O. Cook of Keokuk
Had a bit of business luck,
Bought a passage on a ship,
Round the world he took a trip;
At the world Cook took a look;
The world took one at K. O. Cook.

K. O. Cook of Keokuk
Was completely wonderstruck
When he saw a London cabby,
When he saw Westminster Abbey;
In the Abbey laid to sleep
Mortal tombs immortals keep;
He saw among those holy spots
The tomb of Mary Queen of Scots;
He saw how rare Ben Jonson turns his
Melancholy eyes to Burns's
And many a tomb of marble, such as is
Occupied by Dukes and Duchesses;
His eyes were large and round as saucers
When he came to Geoffrey Chaucer's;
Carven there were all the names
Which the grateful world acclaims;
Therefore, when he found some bad stone
Just above the name of Gladstone,
In his hand a nail he took
And carved the name of K. O. Cook.

K. O. Cook of Keokuk
When in Egypt ran amuck
Carving on the Pyramids
His name and his wife and kids';
Many a humble Arab thinks
K. O. Cook has bought the Sphinx;
Learned scholars who examine
The royal bed of Tut-ankh-amen
By this fact are thunderstruck:
The bed was made in Keokuk!

K. O. Cook of Keokuk
Purchased quite a lot of truck;
Notably a marble tomb
Bigger than his dining-room,
Which upon a hill he stuck
Overlooking Keokuk,
That Keokuk in awe might look
At the tomb of K. O. Cook,
While Cook would lie above the ruck
Looking down on Keokuk.

The hand of death has come to pluck
K. O. Cook of Keokuk;
He lies upon his marble bier;
On the tomb these words appear:
"J. B. Thompson," "Joe Stecchelli,"
"Toledo Skinny," "Mac and Nelly,"
"Picnicked here with grandmamma;
Emma Hay of Omaha."

Nocturne in Blue and Silver

'Tis the dark day's dim ending
   In the old town,
And with the night descending
   Snow drifts down.

The gray of the day surrenders
   To gray of night;
Ah, seek no colored splendors
   In this twilight.

See only the gray snow cover
   With silken shroud
The city, the quiet lover,
   Quiet, proud.

The night dreams long above it,
   Snow falls slow.
"What of it?" you ask, "what of it?"
   I don't know.

We Have Been Here Before

I think I remember this moorland,
　The tower on the tip of the tor;
I feel in the distance another existence;
　I think I have been here before.

And I think you were sitting beside me
　In a fold in the face of the fell;
For Time at its work'll go round in a circle,
　And what is befalling, befell.

"I have been here before!" I asserted,
　In a nook on a neck of the Nile.
I once in a crisis was punished by Isis,
　And you smiled. I remember your smile.

I had the same sense of persistence
　On the site of the seat of the Sioux;
I heard in the teepee the sound of a sleepy
　Pleistocene grunt. It was you.

The past made a promise, before it
　Began to begin to begone.
This limited gamut brings you again. Damn it,
　How long has this got to go on?

Sonnet and Limerick

The sonnet with her Mona Lisa smile
Broods on the world with other-worldly stare.
Priestess of melancholy, darkly fair
Serene above our fury, guilt, and guile,
She, in her deeps, has learned to reconcile
Life's contradictions. Really, I declare,
I'd gladly trust a sonnet anywhere,
That pure, seraphic sedentary. While

The limerick's furtive and mean;
You must keep her in close quarantine,
    Or she sneaks to the slums,
    And promptly becomes
Disorderly, drunk, and obscene.

If Memory Serves

Forgotten, forgotten, forgotten,
    Are the facts that I fain would recall;
My memory always was rotten,
    But now it holds nothing at all.

I always forget what the date is,
    And whom I'm presenting to whom,
What the size of my shirt and my weight is;
    I think I am under a doom.

I forget if I've taken the brake off.
    In a deal, in the brokerage game,
I forgot my legitimate rake-off.
    I'll soon be forgetting my name.

They picked up a chap with amnesia,
    I read in the paper today;
He knew he had been in Rhodesia,
    He talked in a scholarly way;

He knew a few phrases of Finnish;
    He was wearing a little goatee;
His hair was inclined to be thinnish—
    Good gracious! Maybe it's me!

Coriander and Oregano: An Idyll

Rosemary, marjoram, cinnamon, basil—
  Oh, what delightful words to say!
Oh, what sensations, verbal and nasal!
  Savory, juniper, anise, bay!

Who was the poet, who was the paragon—
  He who discovered these names sublime?
Caraway, cardamom, chervil, tarragon,
  Lovage and borage, nutmeg, thyme!

Oh, how delicious the delicate savoring,
  Tongue-tip-tasted on outspread palm
Or merely read in the chapter on flavoring!
  Sesame, saffron, fennel, balm!

How to Treat Elves

I met an elf-man in the woods,
  The wee-est little elf!
Sitting under a mushroom tall—
  'Twas taller than himself!

"How do you do, little elf," I said,
  "And what do you do all day?"
"I dance 'n fwolic about," said he,
  " 'N scuttle about and play;

"I s'prise the butterflies, 'n when
  A katydid I see,
'Katy didn't!' I say, and he
  Says 'Katy did!' to me!

"I hide behind my mushroom stalk
  When Mister Mole comes froo,
'N only jus' to fwighten him
  I jump out 'n say 'Boo!'

" 'N then I swing on a cobweb swing
  Up in the air so high,
'N the cwickets chirp to hear me sing
  'Upsy-daisy-die!'

" 'N then I play with the baby chicks,
  I call them, chick chick chick!
'N what do you think of that?" said he.
  I said, "It makes me sick.

"It gives me sharp and shooting pains
  To listen to such drool."

I lifted up my foot, and squashed
The God damn little fool.

The Immoral Arctic

The Eskimo, explorers state,
    Little regards the marriage vow.
Lightly the bride deceives her mate.
    It makes you sort of wonder how.

Come forth, my love; the Northern Light
    Waves in glory o'er the snow;
We'll dedicate to love this night.
    It's only forty-five below.

Your husband in the igloo snores,
    Heedless of love's adventurers.
Come forth to God's great out-of-doors!
    You'd better put on all your furs.

And it will be sufficient bliss
    To sit and drink your beauty in.
I dare not kiss you, for a kiss
    Is likely to remove the skin.

The Eskimo's incontinence
    Is what the travellers report of.
I don't contest the evidence;
    But still, it makes you wonder, sort of.

United We Sit

In an era
    Long since dead,
Man was here, a
    Quadruped.

Spry enough on
    His all fours,
He was rough on
    Dinosaurs.

He got good and
    Sore and gripèd;
So he stood and
    Was a biped;

Trained his grimy,
    Clumsy hand.
All the time he
    Had to stand.

Now he drinks from
    Wisdom's cup,
But he shrinks from
    Standing up.

Rodin's *Penseur*
    Sits and broods;
He's the sponsor
    For our moods.

We inherit
    Reason's crown;
But we wear it
    Sitting down.

In our vigil
    We proclaim
Feet vestigial;
    They became

Obsolete and
    We forgot 'em.
Farewell, feet, and
    Flourish, bottom!

Answering Yours of (Date Illegible)

The morning mail is here; I have your charming letter;
  I kiss each word you penned, with ecstasy devout;
I love each little word; I'd love them even better
  If I could make them out.

Your writing is as strange and dark as modern art is;
  A rippling, trembling line, with curls and whirls between;
—Alas what news is this! "Flinty," you say my heart is?
  Or "flirty" do you mean?

Inscrutable, the page yields not to my entreaty,
  You speak in covered words of Delphic mystery;
It looks as though you think that I am "such a sweety";
  (Or "sweaty," can it be?)

Can "deary" be the word? I trust it is not "beery,"
  My whispers, not my whiskers, that linger in your ear;
And do you find my verse so cheesy or so cheery?
  And am I deaf or dear?

Your writing swoops and swirls, with no suggestion whether
  I am an Awful Slob or only Awful Slow;
Do you perhaps suggest that we should "roam" together?
  Or is it double o?

My brain resembles now the Battle of Manila,
  Even your signature I study with dismay;
Lola or Lena, Lisa, or Lina, Laura, Lilla—
  Who are you, anyway?

Ozymandias Revisited

I met a traveller from an antique land
Who said: Two vast and trunkless legs of stone
Stand in the desert. Near them on the sand,
Half sunk, a shatter'd visage lies, whose frown
And wrinkled lip and sneer of cold command
Tell that its sculptor well those passions read
Which yet survive, stamp'd on these lifeless things,
The hand that mock'd them and the heart that fed;
And on the pedestal these words appear:
"My name is Ozymandias, king of kings:
Look on my works, ye Mighty, and despair!"
Also the names of Emory P. Gray,
Mr. and Mrs. Dukes, and Oscar Baer
Of 17 West 4th St., Oyster Bay.

If I May Quote

If I may quote: "Professor A
  Says: 'Let me quote Professor B:
"In his inimitable way
  The tale is told by Doctor C:

""" 'The genial Walter de la Mare
  Remarked: "Remember Tom Carlyle?
He said: 'There was a country pair
  Gossipping by a Scottish stile.

""""" "Yestreen," said Jock, "I heard 'ee, lass,
  Gowpin' wi' Robin on the green.
Tha said: ''Twas only Michaelmas
  Tha gave thy troth to blowsy Jean;

" 'For thee," tha said, "my spirit yearns;
  On thee my heart will ever dote!"
Quoth Jean: "To quote from Bobbie Burns:
  'Unquote!'"'"—if I may quote—"""'Unquote!'"'"

Lines Found Scribbled on the Back of a Menu

In the wide banquet dreadfully alone
I watch the jaws that swing upon their hinges,
The upward chump-chump-chumping that impinges
The golden inlay on the enamelled bone.
I watch lips rabbiting the leaves of plants
And folding over scraps of animal tissue.
I hear the little happy sighs that issue
With the consumption of intoxicants.
Now one who stands ejects a current of air
And modulates it in significant sounds.
Brotherhood, concord, union he expounds,
And the good fellowship that men should share.
He speaks the truth; no doubt he speaks the truth.
I have a bit of gristle in my tooth.

Mournful Numbers

Where in the attic the dust encumbers
  Days that are gone,
I found a paper with telephone numbers
  Scribbled thereon.

Again I feel the tremendous wallop
  It gave to me
When I had a valid excuse to call up
  1503.

Again I feel the excuses springing,
  Just as of yore,
When I could no longer refrain from ringing
  9944.

Again I feel my old heart prickle
  As in my youth,
When I left the house to deposit a nickel
  In a sound-proof booth;

And I hear again a phantasmal titter,
  As I would coo
Passionately to the dark transmitter:
  "2342!"

My heart awakes, as if roused from slumber
  By a telephone bell;
Quick! I will call again the number
  Once loved so well!

I breathe the syllables recollected:
  "2342!"

But Central answers: "Disconnected!"
    How true! How true!

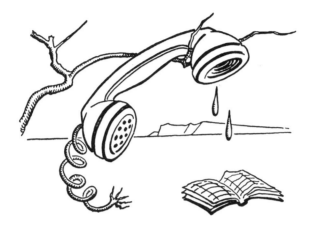

Medical Warnings

"It's getting you," the Doctor said,
  "I warn you for your sake,
It makes the liver quake and quiver,
  Muscles twitch and shake,
It makes the brain grow dull and numb,
  The heart backfire and shirk!"
Said I, "I think you must mean Rum."
  "No," said the Doctor; "Work!"

"You cannot cut it out," he said,
  "But cut it down, I pray;
It burns and gripes your tender pipes
  And takes your wind away;
Heartburn and poison it begets
  And gloom and lassitude."
Said I, "You must mean Cigarettes."
  "No," said the Doctor; "Food!"

"The normal, careful folk," he said,
  "Most quickly pass away;
You aren't robust; I'll give you just
  A month before you pay
The debt that no man may evade!"
  Then I, in agony,
"You mean that Nature must be paid?"
  "No," said the Doctor; "Me!"

On Pelf, or Lucre

When I was young and hearty
　　And full of sap and glee,
I knew a wise old party
　　Who used to say to me:

"Ah, set no store by money,
　　For wealth lasts but a day;
The bees who garner honey
　　Soon see it reft away;

"And greed and grief besmirch us
　　When Lucre is our goal;
And Money cannot purchase
　　A pure and happy soul,

"Or Peace beyond our guessing,
　　Or Love that will not die;
There's many and many a blessing
　　That Money will not buy."

"Money, no doubt, is grimy,"
　　I answered with a bow,
"However, it would buy me
　　All that I need right now.

" 'Twould buy the landlord, maybe,
　　Peace; and Peace for us,
Belly-bands for the baby,
　　And brake-bands for the bus.

"You speak well; but the hitch is
　　That all I ever knew
Who sneered and jeered at riches
　　Were millionaires like you!"

His counsels I neglected;
　　I slaved and strained for pelf

Until I had collected
A million bones myself.

I bear to him no ill-will,
For I have noticed how
My million dollars still will
Buy what I need right now;

And Money brings the right to
Proclaim both near and far
(While someone holds a light to
My fifty-cent cigar):

"Ah, set no store by money————"

Not Unmindful of the Negative as I Am Not . . .

"My sympathy with Mr. Schorer's position is not inconsiderable."
                                        —W. M. Sale in *Epoch.*

Not inconsiderable is the sympathy I share
    With the negative-lovers, a not unplentiful lot;
Yet it is not impossible to be not unaware
    Of the disadvantages of the double and quadruple Not.

The negative fails of being not inexact;
    One Not too many, too few, and what have you got?
Your not innocuous Not will then react!
    If Not's not not, then prithee, what's Not not?

Ah, To Be In . . .

Ah to be in Rarotonga, 'neath the languor-laden breeze,
Or to be in Erromango, in the far New Hebrides!
Ah, to drowze beneath the palm trees on a green Pacific isle,
Where every prospect pleases and where man, besides, is vile!

There is magic in the atlas; how the names allure my eyes!
Ah, to be in Hiddi Birra, where the Jam-jam Mountains rise!
Or Kasongo on the Kongo, where Kibombo gleams afar!
Or in Kilwa Kisiwami, looking north to Zanzibar!

Oh, this life is dull and dreary; I would journey far away
To Jalalabad and Lhasa, to Kabul and Mandalay!
Ah, the Runn of Cutch! Rajpipla! and that dim and ancient land
Where the caravans come shuffling into silken Samarkand!

(There's a lad in old Rajpipla with an atlas in his clutch,
And his dreaming eyes are gazing far beyond the Runn of
            Cutch,
And mysterious music lures him, and he murmurs soft and low,
"Cincinnati! Cincinnati! Buffalo, ah, Buffalo!

"Ah, to be in that far city, blooming like a tropic rose,
Where by golden Allegheny the Monongahela flows;
How sweet the limpid syllables that stir my heart to joy,
As I whisper, 'Ah, Chicago! Fair Chicago, Illinois!'")

What Hath Man Wrought Exclamation Point

Amid Thibetan snows the ancient lama
Mutters his lifelong intercessions comma
Turns the unresting wheel of prayer a myriad
Times in its sacred circling period period
But hold comma what omen strange and dark
Is this on high interrogation mark
A giant bird has out of India stolen
To ravish holy Thibet semicolon
The plane soars upward comma tops the crest
Of the inviolate God of Everest
Period and the lama smote his wheel
Asunder semicolon with a peal
Of dreadful laughter he arose and cried
Colon quotation marks the God has died
Comma so worship man who dared and smote
Exclamation line of dots close quote

Why and How I Killed My Wife

"Nancy," I said, "I would not retail
  Your faults; and yet I cannot fail
To make some mention of a detail———"
  But she corrected me—"detail!"

"My dear," I said, "you're mine, you're *my* Nance,
  You may correct me when, by chance,
I err, with reference to finance———"
  And Nancy smiled and said—"finance!"

"Or when," said I, "I fail to fill a straight,
  When undue odds my purpose frustrate,
Correct me, if with oaths I illustrate———"
  She shook her head and said—"illustrate!"

"Correct my manners or my waggeries,
  But though my accent's not the berries,
Spare my pronunciation's vagaries———"
  To that she merely said—"vagaries!"

"Yes, when you dine," I said, "or when you wine,
  And I grow talkative, why then you win,
For you correct my words so genuine———"
  She said with condescension—"genuine!"

"Think! Every journey, every sea-tour
  Has end; and every ill its cure;
It's a long road that has no detour!"
  Her only comment was—"detour!"

The blood within my veins ran riotous,
  I cried: "No more shall grammar cheat us!"
Take from my vengeful fist your quietus!"
  She moaned in agony—"quietus!"

I whammed her on the cerebellum
Her beating brain to overwhelm;
I hung her body on an elm—
And as she died she whispered—"elm!"

The Man Who Knows the Rules

In muddle and mess and dire distress.
Ere man's dumb anger cools,
Who is the man who saves the day?
The Man Who Knows the Rules!

When the Game halts at challenge of faults,
And venom invades the schools,
Who is it bids us Play the Game?
The Man Who Knows the Rules!

And it's just the same in Life's Great Game;
Who is it ridicules
Our jars and feuds, and peace concludes?
The Man Who Knows the Rules!

Who is it brings the Truth to things,
Making us look like fools?
Who is it gives us a pain in the neck?
The Man Who Knows the Rules!

I Am the Corporal of My Soul

Life's askew
    In most regards;
But I can do
    Tricks with cards.

Men succumb
    To ennui.
Fleas bite some,
    Not me.

Songs are stilled,
    Teeth decay;
Mine were filled
    Yesterday.

'Mid the giggle
    Of the spheres
I can wiggle
    Both my ears.

Doom may smite,
    Fortune flee,
I'm all right;
    I've me.

Lines Composed in Fifth Row Center

Of all the kinds of lecturer
The lecturer I most detest
Is he who finishes a page
And places it behind the rest.

I much prefer the lecturer
Who takes the pages as he finishes
And puts them on a mounting pile
As the original pile diminishes.

But best of all the lecturer
Who gets his papers in confusion
And prematurely lets escape
The trumpet-phrase: "And in conclusion . . ."

The Artists Are Eavesdropping

I've been to the play of the moment,
  The ultimate essence of Art;
The critics averred that the show meant
  That Life has fallen apart.
At the word constituting the climax
  The plaudits increased to a gale.
('Twas the very same word the farmhand used
  When the cow kicked over the pail.)

They showed me a novel, the bible
  Of all that are leading the way
From an art which is local and tribal
  To the glorious art of today.
"Just look at the phrase he has printed!"
  They cried, "What a masterpiece!"
('Twas the very same phrase the barkeep used
  To describe the Chief of Police.)

I met a dear lady, adhering
  To a deep intellectual band;
Her manner was scornful and sneering
  Toward everything I understand.
Without any urging, however,
  A comical ballad she sang.
('Twas the very same song the teamster trolled
  To amuse the construction gang).

The Vanguard impresses me greatly,
  But somehow it seems as though
They've only discovered lately
  What all the rest of us know.
They make me feel like exclaiming:
  (Here you will please insert
The same remark the truckdriver makes
  When a wheel settles deep in the dirt.)

Poetic Five-Finger Exercises

1. Unorthodox Smock-frocks

Wilhelmina Meany has a funny sort of smock-frock
Which the other ladies living up and down the block knock,
Calling it unsightly and a loud and garish hodge-podge
In which all atrocities that you and I would dodge lodge.
So I sought the studio where she among her works lurks;

She was sitting in her smock and reading Edmund Burke's works.
Wondering I gaze upon that paragon of smock-frocks,
Which was advantageously exhibiting her socks' clocks.
"Please," I said, "Miss Meany, though my query may appear
    queer,
Did the inspiration come exclusively from near-beer?
For the madhouse colors and designs assembled pell-mell
Look a little boozy: (sniff!) it surely has a swell smell!"
"What care I," she answered, "if the populace my smock mock!
Though it shocks the orthodox, I'll never hock a smock-frock!"

2. *The Infelicity of Richard Tuttle*

Mary Tuttle cares for knick-knacks,
  And it gives her dreadful shocks
That her coarse-grained husband, Dick, lacks
  Taste, and all her knick-knacks knocks.

He objects to foolish gew-gaws,
  Snorting when she proudly shows
Bits of tin and glass and blue gauze—
  All his gold for gew-gaws goes!

But he has to let her prattle,
  And he dares make no rebuttal;
He would be, if he should tattle,
  Titled "Tittle-Tattle Tuttle"!

3. *Not Much Sense in This*

Said Hatch the fish-etcher
  To Fitch the fish-hatcher,
"I've thought up, I'll betcher,
  A wish which'll catch yer!"

He made his old switch swish,
  And said, "How I wish Fitch
Would hatch in a ditch fish
  Untroubled by fish-itch!"

Said Fitch, "If you dish fish
  Into ditches, they'll twitch, which
Is just what ditch-fish wish.
  Pish! Ditch-fish which itch twitch!"

4. *What Tomasita Taught Her Tutor*

Once a tutor, Peter Potter,
Tutored Tomasita Sautter;
And his love grew hot or hotter
Than the boiling point of water.

Peter sought to be a suitor;
When his proffered hand he brought her
Tomasita taught her tutor
More than e'er the tutor taught her.

For she fled when he besought her,
Lying hid where none would note her;
So a waste of winter water
Would obliterate a bloater.

Tomasita's suitor sought her;
Just in time he chanced to spot her
Ere the Latin quarter caught her,
Ere, perchance, the gutter got her.

Ah, what joy when Tomasita,
Yielding utterly to Potter,
Twittered, "I'm a rotter, Peter!
I reiterate, a rotter!"

Where Is the Je-M'En-Fichisme of Yesterday?

Some thirty years ago
  (More, if you quibble)
The universal *mot*
  Was "ish kabibble."

We let the world go by;
  Its foolish flurry
Evoked the cheery cry
  Of "I should worry."

In that exultant day
  We saw no good of
Worrying life away.
  Perhaps we should've.

Do Good Works, Up to Twenty Per Cent of Adjusted Gross Income

Take all you have, the Bible says, and give it to the poor—
But such a course is sure to leave you somewhat insecure.
Twenty per cent the government considers as the maximum to be deducted on your income tax.

In giving alms, the Bible says, let not your left hand know
The generous donations that your right hand may bestow,
And do your good in secret, and conceal its very tracks—
Then how can you deduct it on your income tax?

And lay not up your treasures in this earthly habitation,
Where moth and rust and burglaries entail depreciation.
There's one consideration that this admonition lacks:
Such losses *are* deducted on your income tax.

Although you take the Bible as the way to get to Heaven, you
Will not impress the officers who guide internal revenue.
So if you buy a Bible, merely read it and relax;
It cannot be deducted on your income tax.
Ho, the income tax! Hey, the income tax!
It cannot be deducted on your income tax!

Community Center

Men'll go kennel
    Themselves in clubs;
The rummy get chummy
    In the bars and pubs;
The ladies and maidies
    Would far rather be
Down in the town in the
    A.&P.

Where broccoli cockily
    Flaunts its sprays,
'Mid liver a-quiver
    On shimmering trays,
'Mid carrots and clarets
    The bourgeoisie
Come in to chum in
    The A.&P.

And then, folks, the men-folks
    Assess with scorn
This prattle and tattle.
    The following morn
They state to the eight-two
    Commuters with glee
Who's in the news in the
    A.&P.

The Great Snow of 1943

So in the midnight the great snow
   Covered over the dark ground;
Feet were hobbled and wheels spun;
   The hydrants smothered, sank, drowned.

The great snow bandaged the street lights,
   And banked the doors of the bright shops,
And hid the hot little cars deep,
   And mounded over the train tops.

Careless and pure, the snow fell.
   This was the finish, we all knew.
So man expired in a white dream.
   It seemed like a damned good idea, too.

The Perforated Spirit

The fellows up in Personnel,
    They have a set of cards on me.
The sprinkled perforations tell
    My individuality.

And what am I? I am a chart
    Upon the cards of IBM;
The secret places of the heart
    Have little secrecy for them.

It matters not how I may prate,
    They punch with punishments my scroll.
The files are masters of my fate,
    They are the captains of my soul.

Monday my brain began to buzz;
    I was in agony all night.
I found out what the trouble was:
    They had my paper clip too tight.

Take Your Tongue Out of Your Cheek and Be Comfortable

An author does not indicate
In article or chronicle
Whether he tells his story straight
Or if he is ironical.

I glumly mutter: "Look at here,
Now are you sly and Byrony,
Or are you bitterly sincere,
Or is it only irony?"

And may I therefore not suggest:
If Irony should swagger in
A text, that it should be expressed
By putting, say a † in?

And when you've had your bit of fun
And pulled your little gag or two,
You ought to show that you have done
By an inverted ⸸ too.

†O goddess of the insincere,
Adorable and sireny!
Permit thy lover to appear
Ironical of Irony! ⸸

Just Off the Concrete

Now by the crossroads, in the filling station,
The boys assemble. Out of the winter night,
Salting the stubbled face, peppering the lungs,
They enter the hot smell of burning wood,
And thawing wool, and heady gasoline.
The radio, the household imbecile,
Slavers and crows unheeded. Pop flows free.
And the old tales are told, born of the earth,
Ripened like grain, and harvested for winter.

It seems the village veterinarian
Suggested to the village constable
A little expedition after rabbits.
The constable, he likes a little shooting,
And so they met up at the doctor's house.
Well, Doc he had some prime old applejack,
And just in case they should get struck by lightning
Or something, why they hit it pretty hard.
Well, they were feeling good when they got started.
And when they drove down past the Weaver place,
The Doc he says: "You see that cow in the pasture?
Bet you five dollars I could hit that cow,
Setting right here." "Well, bet you couldn't!"
The constable he says. And just like that,
The Doc he reaches back and grabs a rifle
Out of the back seat, and he draws a bead.
And drops that cow as dead as butcher meat!
"By gosh, I guess I *did* kill Weaver's cow!"
The Doc says. And "By gosh, I guess you did,
You gol-durn fool!" the cop says. Well, they turned
Around, and bust all records back to town,
And had a couple, quick. The constable
Went to the drug-store, and he bought some gum,
And hung around there all the afternoon,
Establishing, you know, an alibi.
It wasn't hardly evening when the Sheriff
Went to the drug-store. All the boys were there.

And he goes right up to the constable,
And says to him: "Say, Alfred, where was you
At three o'clock this afternoon?" The cop
Says: "I was out to my garage, I guess.
My carbureter, she don't work so good."
"Then you ain't seen the vet?" the Sheriff says.
"No, I ain't seen him, not since yesterday."
"You don't know who went hunting with the vet?"
"Gosh, no. I only know it wasn't me."
"Must have been someone looked a lot like you."
"Well, Judas Priest, they's plenty looks like me."
"Well, I got witnesses they say 'twas you.
You ain't heard nothing then of Weaver's cow?"
"My gosh, I didn't know he had a cow!
I ain't been near the Weaver place today!
I swear I didn't touch his gol-durn cow!
If the vet says I did, I say he lies!
What happened to the durn cow, anyhow?"
"Why," says the Sheriff, "Arthur Weaver says
He had to have her killed, she was so old,
And don't give down no more. And so the vet,
He went and shot her there this afternoon!"
Well, up to town the boys are laughing still.

Drowsiness gathers in the filling station.
Stirring their courage in the warmth and laughter,
The boys turn homeward. On the frozen ruts
Of the hill roads the little cars are shaken.
All the lights cease. The pond-ice cracks with cold.

Sometimes I Feel Like a Left-Handed Neutron

This is the era of the positive negative.
Bodies are by antibodies brought to submission.
The anti-proton converts matter into anti-matter.
Position is nowhere; there is no position.
Time has turned backward; sometimes it goes sidewise.
Timelessness shines with a negative resplendence.
An anti-Columbus will undiscover America,
A non-Jefferson unwrite the Declaration of Independence.

In Nature's Garden

Let's to the meadows, lad; the year's at flood,
And the boon earth persuades the errant foot;
Now the shy bugbane carpets all the wood,
And butterflies kiss their darling pleurisy-root.
And now the world's green smock is gayly smutch'd
With corpse-plant and with foetid camomile,
And nods the jocund pig-sty daisy, which we'd
　　Best leave untouch'd,
Together with the too-fair-seeming itchweed,
That lures the trustful kine with treach'rous smile.

Unhappy kine, that find amid their fodder
Clammy azalea, or rank scorpion grass!
Sweeter the strangleweed or common dodder
(Or love vine). But away! Away! Let's pass
To brighter meads, where wanton louseworts lodge.
Nosebleed and hairy vetch are thick along
Our dancing way, where none shall see us go
　　Save simple Hodge,
Who for a wondering moment stays his hoe,
And open-mouth'd, forgets his country song.

Look Us Over, Posterity

Historians dealing with Mary of Scots
  Grieve and deplore, as is customary,
The lack of materials touching her plots;
  We cannot be sure if we're just to Mary.

The documents' dearth, it is commonly said,
  Interferes with the proper commemorating
Of Cheops, Columbus, and Eric the Red;
  It's a troublesome task to give them a rating.

But the present is aiding the future, at last,
  With newsreels and libraries, fortunately;
Now every suburbanite writes of his past
  In the long afternoons on his porch in Nutley.

The Times has its copies imprinted on rag,
  And no corner-stone is impenetrable
To him who would learn how we blab or we brag
  Of society's shame and our Senate trouble.

We leave to posterity treasures of facts
  To resolve all the legends that grow about us,
And the richest equipment to study our acts—
  But what if it won't want to know about us?

We Should All Be as Happy as Kings

I often think how happy we should feel
That no piranhas in our rivers dwell
Th'unwary bather to devour; no eel
Shoots his electric ire from caudal cell.

Happy, that germs of beer and bread and cheese
Keep their accustomed province, and not yet
Invade our tissues with a fell disease;
Happy, that violets smell of violet;

Happy, that ozone in our atmosphere
Repels the murd'rous zeal of cosmic ray.
There was another reason, too; it's queer,
I cannot seem to think of it today.

A Salute to the Modern Language Association,
Convening in the Hotel Pennsylvania

The Modern Language Association
    Meets in the Hotel Pennsylvania
And the suave Greeters in consternation
    Hark to the guests indulging their mania

For papers on "Adalbert Stifter as the Spokesman of
        Middle-Class Conservatism,"
    And "The American Revolution in the *Gazette de Leyde* and the
        Affaires de l'Angleterre et de l'Amérique,"
And "Emerson and the Conflict Between Platonic and Kantian
        Idealism,"
    And "Dialektgeographie and Textkritik,"

And "Vestris and Macready: Nineteenth-Century Management at
        the Parting of the Ways,"
    And "Pharyngeal Changes in Vowel and Consonant
        Articulation,"
And "More Light on Molière's Theater in 1672–73, from *Le
        Registre* d'Hubert, Archives of the Comédie Française,"
    And "Diderot's Theory of Imitation."

May culture's glossolalia, clinging
    In Exhibit Rooms and Parlor A,
Sober a while the tempestuous singing
    Of fraternal conventions, untimely gay;

May your influence quell, like a panacea,
    A business assembly's financial fevers,
With the faint, sweet memory of "Observaciones sobre la
        aspiración de H en Andalucía,"
    And "The Stimmsprung (Voice Leap) of Sievers."

You Too Can Conquer Your Better Nature

My father once bestowed on me a dollar,
Rewarding some good deed I had not done.
Should I accept? I struggled with my scruples.
And I won.

My courage once was publicly commended—
I had stood fast, too paralyzed to run.
Should I tell all? I fought my better nature;
And I won.

When conscience bade me make a full confession,
Repenting every tawdry fault and sin,
I fought a war with conscience; and I won it.
I always win.

A Booklovers' Bargain

"Shame!" said the writer's wife, and her voice shook;
  "And would you put each intimate word and deed
Of our common life in the pages of a book
  For all the world to read?

"All our sweet secrets, would you write them down?
  The murmured words of love's confessional,
Shall they be shouted to the gaping town?
  Have you no shame at all?"

The writer fidgeted before his wife,
  And muttered from his overladen heart:
"I got to get material from life!
  I got to think of Art!"

"Then think of Art!" she blazed; "No more of me!
  No more shall you abuse me to another!
Offer my inmost life to your deity!
  I shall return to Mother!"

The writer wept; in vain did he beseech,
  In vain assail the cloak of wrath that wrapped her.
He made some notes upon her farewell speech
  For his concluding chapter.

Ah well! Let the heart break—'tis the world's gain!
  Beauty from blood will grow, like Flanders poppies.
The world, in gratitude for the author's pain,
  Bought just three hundred copies.

Merry Old Souls

Old Ben Franklin was a merry old soul,
He walked up Market Street munching on a roll,
And a girl laughed loud, and her laughter was so ranklin'
That Old Ben Franklin made her Mrs. Ben Franklin.

Old Julius Caesar was a merry old soul,
To be a Roman Emperor was all his goal.
But he put away the crown; he was such an old teaser
That the mob put the finger on Caius Julius Caesar.

Old Isaac Newton was a merry old soul,
He invented gravitation when out for a stroll;
And no one up to now has succeeded in refutin'
The good old hypothesis of Old Isaac Newton.

Rabelais also was a merry old soul;
Many of his writings are very very droll;
Censors in the custom-house treat him rather shabbily
By cutting out the better bits of Master Francis Rabelais.

"Towanda Winooski? Gowanda!"
Rahway Setauket Eugene.
"Watseka? Ware! Tonawanda!"
Flushing Modesto De Queen.

"Wantagh Malone Petaluma!
Pontiac! Rye! Champaign!
Kissimmee Smackover! Yuma!"
Ossining, Waverly Kane.

"Rockaway! Homestead Tacoma!
Neenah Metuchen Peru!
Owego Moberly Homer!
Dover Andover Depew!"

Listen Here, Capital and Labor

Hearken to me, O Capital and Labor!
This is no time for quarrels and scraps.
Let's all get together like one big neighbor—
Capital and Labor, you deaf perhaps?

Now bushelmen, bushel, and bakers, bake;
Sturdily cast, ye casters on slush;
Stripper-opaquers, strip, opaque;
Ye offset tuschers, tusch, tusch!

Let the ideal of production illumine
The soul of director, mechanic, clerk.
Let us heed the words of ex-President Truman
And dedicate all of our strength to work.

So pullers and wringermen, speed your wringers;
Octopus fishers, catch octopus;
And fingerwavers, wave your fingers;
Bus boys, bus girls, buss, buss.

Be earnest! Be firm! Be enthusiastic!
Till a hundred million cars are loose
On the roads, till we're up to our waists in plastic.
Never you mind. Produce! Produce!

Address, addressograph operators;
Jolly recappers, recap, recap;
And cure, curates; curate, curators;
Purse, pursers; lappers, lap.

New Light on the Hen

The aboriginal hen
  Was a wild and fearsome beast;
She lived in trees with chimpanzees
  In the mysterious East:

The hen's ferocious cackle
  Stilled the woods with fear;
And scholars say she did not lay
  A dozen eggs a year.

But aboriginal man
  (The scholars do aver)
Entrapped the hen, and patient men
  Domesticated her.

They brought her out of the woods
  Into the sunshine clear,
And were repaid, because she laid
  Some sixty eggs a year.

And now we've gone and found
  The ultra-violet ray;
The hens blaspheme its constant gleam,
  But lay and lay and lay.

With artificial sun
  A hen will volunteer
(I understand) three hundred and
  Forty eggs a year!

But what is this I read?
  Now all physicians say
That you and I have got to try
  The ultra-violet ray!

We've got to strip and sit
  In the ultra-violet glare!
O fellow-men, remember the hen!
  Beware! Beware! Beware!

Spring

Now rouses Earth, so long quiescent,
  To kiss and curse her fate,
In storm of bliss or woe incessant,
  Despairing or elate.
She's only being adolescent;
  Nothing to do but wait.

Flowers of Rhetoric

I grant you there is much excuse
For simile and metaphor,
But moderation in their use
I'd wage a small vendetta for.

They gleam amid the puffing prose
Of Art's advanced minorities
(As on the maiden's bosom glows
The symbol of sororities

(Which bind with bonds like linkèd brass
(As sturdy as austerity
(Which irritates like mustard gas
(Which spreads like insincerity

(Elusive as a synonym
(Which flees away like Saracens
(Who fought in battles vague and dim
As most of these comparisons.)))))))

So everything's like something else
In these new-fangled rhetorics.
But I'll resist 'em (like the Celts
And hopeless Vercingetorix).

Arcadia Mixture

I wonder where I could get some genuine carpet slippers,
And a fez, and a red velvet smoking jacket (not flannel),
And a brass coal hod with cannel coal for my grate,
And a grate for my cannel.

Slippered and fezzed by my grate, I would smoke a calabash
    pipe
And read Anthony Trollope all the livelong day,
And I would exclaim at intervals, "Bang away, world!
Bang away, bang away!"

Don't Knock, and It Shall Be Opened unto You

On a nearby campus a new library rises;
Its entrance controlled by electric eyes is.
When a scholar approaches the right-hand door
There is no necessity to smite and/or
Push; for it yawns before him dramatically.
And for exit, the left-hand door gapes automatically.

Now by the campus dogs this delightful fact is
Discovered; and the livelong day their practice
Is to run in at the right-hand door, spin around inside,
And gallop out the left-hand door, opening wide.
With glad barks of boxers, airedales, and hounds
The Shrine of Wisdom constantly resounds.

May we not perceive in this circumstance a parable?
No doubt to hide away learning is terrible,
But to open it up wide electronically is bad too,
For few attain wisdom unless they have had to
Struggle. The scholars aver (I have quizzed 'em)
There's a frightful draft in the Shrine of Wisdom.

The Impact of Beriberi on Walla Walla, Wash.

All the folks who live in Walla Walla
    Love to execute the hula-hula,
Love to sing the ancient Eli Eli,
    Strangely harmonized with Boola-Boola.

Commonly their expletive is "Tut-tut!"
    And they like their garments with a froufrou,
Like to play a tomtom in a putt-putt,
    Call for chowchow, dining on the choo-choo.

Though they dose themselves with agar-agar,
    They are rather prone to beriberi.
Are they apprehensive? Not so very;
    As they put it, "Not so very very."

Diogenes

Diogenes lived in a tub,
Eating the plainest of grub;
And eminent people he'd snub.
He apparently did it for pub-
　　　licity.

Alexander the Great had the whim
To call; he looked over the rim
Of the tub. But the scholar was grim;
And "Kindly move out of my glim!"
Was all to be got out of him;
Which was thought at the time to be sim-
　　　plicity.

But what he was after, we know,
Was to get people talking, and so
To make his philosophy go,
And make the world conscious of sto-
　　　icity.

And what were the views of this cub?
Well, really, you know, there's the rub.
I cannot recall, like a dub.
But I know that he lived in a tub!
And there is the trouble with pub-
　　　licity!

A Tonversation with Baby

"Was it a little baby
     With wide, unwinking eyes,
Propped in his baby carriage,
     Looking so wise?

"Oh, what a pwitty baby!
     Oh, what a sweety love!
What is oo thinkin', baby,
     And dweamin' of?

"Is oo wond'rin' 'bout de doggie
     A-fwiskin' here 'n dere?
Is oo watchin' de baby birdies
     Everywhere?

" 'N all de funny peoples
     'N a funny sings oo sees?
What is oo sinkin of, baby?
     Tell me, please.

" 'Z oo sinkin of tisses, tunnin,
     'N wannin 'n wannin for some?
O tweety goo swummy doodle,
     O yummy yum!"

Then spoke that solemn baby,
     Wise as a little gnome:
"You get in the baby carriage;
     I'll push you home."

Memory Rhyme To Be Sung
While Packing the Suitcase

First the evening shoes, and slippers
In their dainty bags with zippers.
Lay the pearly shirts beside,
Gleaming in their candid pride.
Pack the gaps with underclothes
And socks (and check the heels and toes.)
Handkerchiefs, pajamas, ties
Shall be used to equalize.
Leave a just-sufficient space
For the bloated toilet-case.
On the surface now dispose,
Tenderly, the evening clothes.
Stop! Unhappy who forgets
To include some cigarettes,
Evening collar, studs, and socks.
It is finished. Snap the locks.
(Don't forget the bag.) Depart
With a high and tranquil heart.

And returning, roll it all
Tight together in a ball.

The Contortionists' Tragedy

The Artist sits alone upon a pinnacle
   Whereto the vulgar world may not attain.
The Artist often gets extremely cynical
   Regarding human passion, human pain;
Or so, at least, would frequently insist
   The winsome Artist, Angela Tremaine,
Who, at the age of twenty, was unkissed,
   For to her Art her life was dedicated.
She was an eminent contortionist.

But on a day above all others fated
She met a youth with burning eyes aglow.
   "So pleased to meet you!" he politely stated,
And swiftly took his hat off with his toe.
   'Twas the contortionist, McDowell Biddle.
Angela's pulses hammered; bowing low,
   She wound herself into a human riddle;
Her head passed 'twixt her legs, and then appeared,
   Smiling self-consciously, above her middle.
Their hands clasped, winding in a manner weird.
   "You are the girl I've sought since babyhood!"
He cried; and suddenly their lips adhered
   (As well as, in their tanglement, they could)
And Life and Art for them were reconciled,
   Both understanding, and both understood.

So they were wedded, and the heavens smiled,
   And for a space they lived in fairyland.
With many a frolic was their life beguiled;
   Coquettishly she'd flee his petful hand
And twine herself about the chandelier,
   While he would jacknife in th' umbrella stand,
Or from the icebox would he quaintly peer.
   Ah, firstling happiness, too fond, too fleeting!
Angela, insufficiently austere,
   Listened too calmly to the soft entreating
Of virtuosos on the melodious saw,
   Or to the amorous piccolo-player's bleating.

And jealousy in Biddle's heart did gnaw,
  Suspecting, reconciled, again suspicious;
And Angela would fleck him on the raw,
  Salting his wounds with mockery malicious,
Until his smould'ring heart could brook no more.
  He sprang upon her, and his snarl was vicious!
She struck at him; they struggled on the floor,
  Twined like the famed Laocoön of stone.
He seized a dagger; and he poised it o'er
  Her bosom; and he cried in horrid tone:
"Now drink of death, thy final loving-cup!"
  But plunged the blade, by error, in his own
Bosom! Contortionists get so mixed up.

Cut Camera, Cut Sound!

"It was months before I knew when to Dissolve and when to Fade."
—Stephen Longstreet
in the Authors League Bulletin

When to Dissolve? And when to Fade?
How may the actors know
The ending of the masquerade,
The wavering shadow-show?

Only the grim Director knows;
The Script in his gripe.
And He may bid the drama close
With the pronouncement: "Wipe!"

The Morality of the Villain

What has become of the villain
    Who swaggered through all the old plays,
Who used to put most of the thrill in
    The drama of earlier days?
The plays of today have reformed him,
    He tries to behave as he should;
The villain is not very bad any more,
    And the hero is not very good!

The villain of old would not wrestle
    With scruples that tortured his brain
As he tied a fair maid to a trestle
    In the path of a limited train;
He would laugh with a laugh diabolic
    As he sandbagged his prey from behind;
But the villain is not very cruel any more,
    And the hero is not very kind!

The villain was thoroughly evil,
    And wicked as long as awake;
His morals were those of a weevil,
    His manners were those of a snake;
To death and despair and disaster
    His innocent victims he'd lure—
But the villain is not very foul any more,
    And the hero is not very pure!

Alas, he is gone; for our time is
    Too wise for such simple demands;
We now have discovered that crime is
    The result of malfunctioning glands;
But still I regret the old villain
    And the hero's damfoolhardihood—

For Vice doesn't seem very bad any more,
And Virtue is not very good!

Something Should Be Done about the Muses

As if I didn't have enough to worry about,
    I got to worrying about the Muses.
Even their names I was a little blurry about;
    True, they are designations one infrequently uses.

I have no actual quarrel with Clio, Terpsichore,
    Or even Urania, Muse of Astronomy.
It doesn't require any particular trickery
    To fit them into our modern economy.

But Calliope, Muse of Epic Poetry! Who now
    Writes epic poems? They've dropped to their minima!
Only in Hollywood are Epics in view now,
    So let's make Calliope Muse of the Cinema.

And Erato, Muse of Erotic Poetry! Shame
    On Erato and on all those whom her screeds amuse!
Let us, rather, give to Erato an honest name
    As Muse of Television, and by golly it needs a Muse.

East Is East and West Is West
and the Twain Have Apparently Met

Here where the Mohawk plied
　　His secret sullen paddle,
The bold Dude Ranchers ride,
　　Uncertain in the saddle.

Oh, it's East I would be in the wide wild spaces,
　　East on the old Frontier,
Where the invoice clerk on his pinto races
　　To bulldog the sulky steer;
East, where the typists ride cayuses,
　　East, where the mustangs neigh,
And the lariat catches in firs and spruces,
　　Ki-yi-yippy-yippy-yay!

In the astonished shade
　　Of elm and maple branches
Canters the gay parade
　　From Adirondack ranches.

Then hi for the old York State arroyo,
　　Hi-ee for chaps and quirt,
And the good old Stetson hat, oh, boy-oh,
　　And the good old purple shirt,
And the cocktail lounge and the old Fun Foreman,
　　And the band of the Lazy K,
And the piny tang of the cowboy doorman!
　　Ki-yi-yippy-yippy-yay!

The Crusty Professor's Song

Once in days of yore
All the college scholars
Resolutely swore
To give up stand-up collars.
Students never wore
Stand-up collars, stand-up collars,
Never any more.

They discarded cuff-links,
And the cuffs likewise;
They abandoned tie-pins
And dispensed with ties.
Students never wore
Cuff-links, cuffs, tie-pins, ties,
Stand-up collars, stand-up collars,
Never any more.

They rejected headgear,
Threw away their hats,
Eliminated garters,
Extirpated spats.
Students never wore
Caps and hats, garters, spats,
Cuff-links, cuffs, tie-pins, ties,
Stand-up collars, stand-up collars,
Never any more.

They renounced the jacket,
They abjured the vest;
They undid the buttons
To display the chest.
Students never wore
Jackets, coats, waistcoats, vests,
Caps and hats, garters, spats,
Cuff-links, cuffs, tie-pins, ties,
Stand-up collars, stand-up collars,
Never any more.

Maybe time will banish
    Sweat-shirts, dirty jeans;
Maybe these will vanish
    From collegiate scenes.
Students will not wear
    Dirty sweat-shirts, dirty jeans,
    Jackets, coats, waistcoats, vests,
    Caps and hats, garters, spats,
    Cuff-links, cuffs, tie-pins, ties,
Stand-up collars, stand-up collars—
    Then what *will* they wear?

The Woman of the Dentist's Dreams

"Women!" the dentist cried, "They are to me
    The mystical far creatures of my dreams,
More pure and fair than earthly men can be,
    Woven of gossamer and pale moonbeams—
Open a little wider, please, the jaw."
He thrust six fingers in the lady's maw.

"'Are you quite real, angelic one,' I say
    To her who is to be ere long my bride,
'Or some dim vision, not of mortal clay?'
    Don't bite, please. Here, the basin at your side.
Woman, our heaven-sent guide, our sweet consoler!
Extreme decay about the second molar.

"Woman, who leaves the skies, a happy martyr,
    With trailing clouds of glory still begirt,
Half elf, half spirit—um, a lot of tartar.
    It looks to me like trench mouth. This will hurt——"
He felt her tongue and epiglottis flutter
Forming fierce curses which she could not utter.

Tell Me, Is Your Ful-Vue Shur-On?

"Silent Nite, Holy Nite—"
If you say: "That looks alrite",
You're sick with advertisingese,
You read without demur: "styl-eez",
You tease your taste with Dain-T-spred,
Your thumb-tacks have a saf-T-hed.
But who would gladly overthrow
The ranks of Cheez-It and Moon-glo?
Let him kum kwik, I mean come quick,
And strike a blow for rhetoric!
We'll form a mighty organization
And advertise for Ed-U-K-shun!

A Short Course in Stoicism

The stoic says the universe
  Is leagued to try the sage's virtue.
If evil smites you, look for worse,
  And if it hurts you, let it hurt you.

Let Nature, with its crowd of woes,
  In vain endeavor to defeat us;
Impassive, let us bear its blows
  Like Seneca and Epictetus.

I met a stoic in a bar
  Who argued much for resignation.
He pushed the stoic faith so far
  That he proposed a demonstration.

"I'm tough," he said, "and I defy
  Fate's angry effort to provoke me.
I'll take a breath, and any guy
  Can hit me. Step right up and poke me!"

But no one present wanted much
  A demonstration so heroic.
Fell circumstance refused to clutch.
  I never saw a madder stoic.

The Gay Nineties

Ho! the comic Nineties!
  Ha! the funny skirts!
Oho! Oho! the silly hats,
  The collars and the shirts!
Weren't our fathers killing,
  Playing at croquet!
Weren't the Nineties too absurd!
  But weren't they gay!

Ha! the architecture!
  Ho! the pointed shoes!
Tee-hee! Tee-hee! the table-talk's
  Conventional taboos!
The things that daddy didn't
  Do! And what was done!
Nevertheless he seemed to have
  A lot of fun.

Isn't it a mercy
  That the Nineties passed?
That the frantic Twenties move
  Forty times as fast?
Don't you pity daddy
  For living long ago?
Haven't we got all the luck?
  No.

Epitaph for a Funny Fellow

He always was one for a jeer and a jest,
  And was given to iconoclasm;
His smile was sardonic, and seemed to suggest:
  "Let others arouse 'em; I razz 'em!"

His phrases were likely to smolder and scald,
  And act like a blister to bluster;
By the name of "buffoon" he was commonly called,
  Though possibly "jester" were juster.

We recently met; he was clouded in gloom;
  His spirit was battered, embittered.
He asked me to chisel these words on his tomb:
  "The universe tottered; I tittered."

Decline and Fall of the Cad

There used to be a cad about,
  And he was quite a wooer,
A spooner and a gadabout,
  A biller and a cooer;
And though his business went to smash,
  He married. I must add,
His wife was forced to work for cash!
  He was a proper cad!

There was a dandiprat about,
  A cad by definition.
He smoked, while ladies sat about,
  And did not ask permission!
The ladies sniffed, the ladies snuffed,
  But little did he heed.
Upon his cigarette he puffed!
  He was a cad indeed!

But now, when people meet about,
  I hear no more: "Egad, sir,
No bushes I will beat about,
  But you, sir, are a cad, sir!"
And if the words should be expressed
  To many a modern lad,
The only answer they'd suggest
  Is "Pray, sir, what's a cad?"

"Was I too hearty? Did he think me bold?
Should I have said, 'like hell,' and not 'like fun'?
Does my mustache not make me look too old?
(He wants a man whose graduate work is done.)
Nebraska Wesleyan is probably cold,
I'd rather get down south of Washington.
He didn't seem to like that joke I told;
Jeez, he's a solemn-looking son of a gun!"
Thus the young savant ponders at his ease,
Knitting the critical brow, and on the belly
Twirling the scholarly thumb, while Ph.D's
Deal with the manuscripts of Machiavelli,
The intervocalic N in Portuguese,
And the unfaithfulness of Harriet Shelley.

The Practice Baby

He was a wee, wee baby, plucked from the heart of a rose,
With tiny clutching hands and feet and a tiny snubbly nose,
With the lips and eyes of a valentine, and a smile from the
    Sunday comics;
He was the Practice Baby in a College of Home Economics.

And every day the Practice Class in Model Baby-Handling
Would give him a Scientific Bath and do some Model Dandling,
And dress him in Model Baby-Clothes and give him a Model
    Kiss,
Or else a Practice Spanking if he behaved amiss.

"Oh, what a lucky baby I am!" he often used to cry,
"To have a hundred Mammas to make me hushaby!
A hundred lovely Mammas, whose love is overflowing!"
The only difficulty was, the baby kept on growing.

And now he's grown to be a man, and grievously he misses
The care of his Model Mammas, their cuddling and their kisses;
And oft he murmurs to himself, with his scowl from the Sunday
    comics:
"Do they need a Practice Husband in the College of Home
    Economics?"

(The "idea," as it is called in the profession, suggested by J. F. Mason)

Ambition

I got pocketed behind 7X-3824;
He was making 65, but I can do a little more.
I crowded him on the curves, but I couldn't get past,
And on the straightaways there was always some truck coming
 fast.
Then we got to the top of a mile-long incline
And I edged her out to the left, a little over the white line,
And ahead was a long grade with construction at the bottom,
And I said to the wife, "Now by golly I got'm!"
I bet I did 85 going down the long grade,
And I braked her down hard in front of the barricade,
And I swung in ahead of him and landed fine
Behind 9W-7679.

Freedom from Speech

I said to Dr. Wilbur Slade:
"Why do you wear a hearing aid?
Your keenness does not fail, I hope?
You did not need a stethoscope;
You laid your ear on terra firma
And sensed an earthquake out in Burma.
You heard a pin drop in the lobby,
And said: 'A safety, not a bobby!'
I grant I am a bit dismayed
To see you wear a hearing aid."

Said Dr. Wilbur Slade to me:
"The apparatus that you see
Is not an Aid, but an Arrester.
I turn the switch; the sorry jester
Recites to deafened ears the wry jest
Culled from the current Reader's Digest.
With this machine I overthrow
The power of public radio.
And with it I need fear no more
The cocktail party's monstrous roar,
The epic of the funny dream,
The arch reproach, the winsome scream,
The tale of How I Earned Success,
The stream of tipsy consciousness.
And chiefly I may now ignore:
'And will there really be a war?' "

"And yet," I said to Dr. Slade,
"Are you not trying to evade
Participation in the fight?
And do you think that this is right?"
A little clicking sound I heard.
"I cannot hear a single word;
Yell if you like," said Dr. Slade.
He patted his Unhearing Aid.

The Roadside Litterateur

There's a little old fellow and he has a little paintpot,
And a paucity of brushes is something which he ain't got,
And when he sees a road sign, the road sign he betters,
And expresses of himself by eliminating letters.

Thus THROUGH ROAD
Becomes ROUGH ROAD
And CURVES DANGEROUS
Is transformed to CURVES ANGER US
And 24-HOUR SERVICE
Turns into 24-HOUR VICE
And MEN AT WORK IN ENTRANCE
Is reduced to MEN AT WORK IN TRANCE
And SLOW DOWN BRIDGE ONE WAY
Is triumphantly condensed to
LOW DOWN BRIDE ON WAY

But the little old fellow feels a slight dissatisfaction
With the uninspiring process of pure subtraction.
The evidence would indicate he's taken as his mission
The improvement of the road signs by the process of addition.

Thus TRAFFIC LIGHT AHEAD
Becomes TRAFFIC SLIGHT AHEAD
And GAS AND OIL
Is improved to GASP AND BOIL
And simple REST ROOMS
Appear as QUEEREST ROOMS
And UNDERPASS ONE WAY
Emerges as UNDERPASS GONE AWAY
And (perhaps his masterpiece)
RIGHT
EAST   BOUND
TUNNEL

Is elaborated to

FRIGHTENED
BEASTS ABOUND
IN TUNNEL

Thus we see how the critical mood
Becomes the creative attitude.

Phaëthon

Apollo through the heavens rode
In glinting gold attire;
His car was bright with chrysolite,
His horses snorted fire.
He held them to their frantic course
Across the blazing sky.
His darling son was Phaëthon,
Who begged to have a try.

"The chargers are ambrosia-fed,
They barely brook control;
On high beware the Crab, the Bear,
The Serpent round the Pole;
Against the Archer and the Bull
Thy form is all unsteeled!"
But Phaëthon could lay it on;
Apollo had to yield.

Out of the purple doors of dawn
Phaëthon drove the horses;
They felt his hand could not command,
They left their wonted courses.
And from the chariot Phaëthon
Plunged like a falling star—
And so, my boy, no, no, my boy,
You cannot take the car.

A Winter Madrigal

Chloris made my heart to stop
And turn'd my joy to acid,
For I was working in the shop
And she was in Lake Placid.

In my despair I could not bear
Her gladsome letters, prating
Of frolic in the sparkling air,
And skiing, sleighing, skating.
Hey nonny, nonny, etc.

It fill'd my soul with woe and hate
To hear about her ski-jumps,
For in proportion to her weight
She jump'd far as a flea jumps;

But now the dart has ceas'd to smart,
My pain has ceas'd to rankle,
For though my Beauty broke my heart
My Beauty broke her ankle.
Hey nonny, nonny, etc.

Somebody's Been Parking in My Parking Space

Dour in the parking lot,
   I sought a white-rimmed oblong
To be my resting spot.
   I did not grieve and sob long;
My fancy seemed to trace
   A message on the pave—
That every parking space
   Is a horse's grave.

Memorial pillars lift
   Beside the plots of asphalt;
To make no votive gift
   Is thought to be a crass fault.
I drop a nickel in,
   And shed a plaintive tear
For the horse who could have been,
   Whose soul is here.

And is he tranquil, then,
   Beneath the black bitumen?
Or will his race again
   Have dealings with the human?
Out of oblivion
   The words materialize:
"When all your gas is gone,
   I will arise!"

Lullaby, Little Adult

The New Statesman and Nation has been offering prizes for verses calculated to bring sleep to sufferers from insomnia.

Forlorn, the bulbul babbles;
  Bereft, the sybil sings;
The dreaming dove bedabbles
  His wayward wings.

No more the rose in sorrow
  Ogles the oriole;
No murmur of the morrow
  Moves the mole.

O wallow, wallow, wallow,
  Where the wan willows loom!
O follow! holloa! swallow!
  Goom; goom.

Thoughts on Rereading "Don Juan"

The reprobate pursues the virtuous woman
  With purposes extremely reprehensible;
He swoops upon his prey as with a Grumman
  Jet plane. To this she cannot be insensible.
I loathe the reprobate; there is no room in
  My mind to make defense of th'indefensible.
Yet surely any scientist of stature'll
Admit the reprobate's behavior's natural.

Then fie on Nature, which approves begetters
  Of by-blows! Let us rather give our plaudit
To blameless men adjusting carburetors,
  To auditors in agony of audit,
To red-eyed commentators on belles-letters,
  To the bank's guards 'gainst crooks who would defraud it,
To those who cheat the grinning doom pursuing 'em
By pressing pants, and advertising chewing gum.

Old Folks at the Home

I often say to an elderly man,
    "What, sir, have *you* found out?"
I whisper it into his hearing aid;
    Sometimes I have to shout.

"I have found out," says an elderly man,
    "Three ways of darning socks."
Another replies, "My message is: Never
    Invest in streetcar stocks."

Another has learned why elderly men
    Sigh when they sit; or maybe
One has discovered why women laugh
    Whenever they see a baby.

Mostly, however, an elderly man
    Huddles within his shawl,
And all he can say to my question is
    "Nothing. Nothing at all."

Who'd Be a Hero (Fictional)?

When, in my effervescent youth,
   I first read "David Copperfield,"
I felt the demonstrated truth
   That I had found my proper field.
As David, simple, gallant, proud,
   Affronted each catastrophe,
Involuntarily I vowed,
   "That's me!"

In Sherlock Holmes and Rastignac
   Much of myself was realized;
In Cyrano de Bergerac
   I found myself idealized.
Where dauntless hardihood defied
   The wrong in doughty derring-do,
I periodically cried,
   "That's me too!"

The lads of Bennett, Wells, and Co.
   Confronted many a thwarting thing,
But well-intentioned, fumbling, slow,
   They tried to do the sporting thing;
And some would nurse a carking shame,
   Hiding the smart from other men.
They often caused me to exclaim,
   "That's me again!"

The fiction of the present day
   I view with some dubiety;
The hero is a castaway,
   A misfit to society,
A drunkard or a mental case,
   A pervert or a debauchee.
I murmur with a sour grimace,
   "Where's me?"

Out Etna Way

       At Etna in the valley
         The woods assemble thick
       About the filling station
         At the bend of the creek;
       The woods invade the clearings,
         The houses all are old;
       And at the filling station
         Old tales are told.

There was a farmer's kid was selling shiners
(The little minnies that you use for bait);
He put a sign up at his father's stand:
"Shiners for sale—a dozen, fifteen cents."
Well, a big car pulled up beside the stand.
"Bud, let me have a look at them there shiners,"
The driver says. "They're mighty pretty shiners.
I'll take a dozen; here's your fifteen cents."
He took a dozen in a Mason jar,
And then he says: "Say, bud, you got a license
For selling bait? Just look at this here star!
I'm the game warden!" "Well, I guess I have!"
And the kid pulls the license from his pants.
The dumb game warden then he hums and haws,
And says: "Say, bud, now come to think of it,
I couldn't use these shiners after all.
I tell you what I'll do; I'll sell 'em back."
"Gee, mister, I don't guess I want 'em back;
I got more shiners now that I can sell."
Then the game warden hummed and hawed some more,
And says: "I'll let you have 'em for a dime."
"No, I don't guess I want 'em," says the kid.
"A nickel, then." The kid he says all right,
And paid the nickel, took the shiners back.
All of a sudden then the young kid's pa
Jumped out from round the corner of the barn
Where he'd been listening. "Hey, mister!" yells
The young kid's pa. "I want to see your license
For selling shiners!" "I don't need no license,

I'm the game warden!" "It don't cut no ice
What all you be. I know that it's the law
You can't sell bait without you got a license!"
Then the kid's pa went up into the house
And telephoned the Justice of the Peace.
And the next day the Justice of the Peace
Put a ten-dollar fine onto the warden.
And the game warden he'd have sure felt cheap
If you could ever cheapen a game warden.

All your great cities,
    Rich and haughty now,
Will be rust and rubble
    Under the plow
Turn the cities under,
    To manure the loam.
The Etna filling station
    Is older than Rome.

Ouch! A Thought Struck Me!

A poet thinks little round thoughts
   weighing no more than an ounce.
You can put four or five in your pocket;
   the important thing is, they bounce.

The novelist thinks large thoughts
   extending from door to door.
They are colored, lumpy, and streaky,
   they dribble all over the floor.

My thoughts, they are curly and frail,
   they will not remain on the ground,
they blow away like potato
   chips over Long Island Sound.

The World of Tomorrow

The Town of Tomorrow is built upon faith and the mud of the
    marshes of Flushing,
    Flushing;
The Town of Tomorrow's excessively smug and boasts in a
    manner unblushing,
    Unblushing-O.
The Town of Tomorrow is morally pure, in the realm that its
    pinnacles smile on,
    Smile on;
For who would get tight in a Plaza of Light, or sin in the shade
    of a Trylon,
    Trylon, Trylon-O?

The World of Tomorrow will rise on its plan, its avenues golden
    and glimmering,
    Glimmering;
The World of Tomorrow will gleam like a jewel with
    sweet-odored fountains a-shimmering,
    Shimmering, shimmering.
In the World of Tomorrow the slum will be doomed and the
    causes of misery paralyzed,
    Paralyzed;
And evil and wrong will pass like a song, and a lot of you folks
    will be sterilized,
    Sterilized, sterilized-O.

Il Penseroso and L'Allegro

"Oh, little is the span
Of ill-starred man,"
  The man who sells insurance
    Said to me;
"Brief our respite, brief
As the hour of the leaf
  That hangs in doubtful durance
    On the tree.
Into the bolted room
Comes doom, comes doom,
  To bring the end allotted
    Of our years;
And what consoles a wife
Except Straight Life?"
  The policy was blotted
    With his tears.

"Unless you would like an annuity
And always enjoy superfluity!
Hippity-high, never say die,
But flourish in gay perpetuity!
A fig for the cares of mortality!"
He foamed with extreme geniality.
"Fol-de-rol-day, your signature, pray—
It is only a little formality!"

There's Money in Mother and Father

The lamp burns long in the cottage,
    The light shines late in the shop,
Their glimmer disclosing the writers composing
    Memories of Mom and Pop.

Oh don't write a book about Poppa!
    Don't write a book about Dad!
Better not bother to tell how Father
    Went so amusingly mad!
Better pass over the evening
    Father got locked in the zoo—
For your infant son has possibly begun
    A funny little book about you!

The author broods in his study,
    The housewife dreams in her flat;
Since Mommer and Popper were most improper,
    There ought to be a book in that!

But don't write a book about Mother!
    Don't write a book about Mum!
We all know Mumsy was vague and clumsy,
    Dithering, drunken, and dumb.
There may be money in Mother,
    And possibly a movie too—
But some little mite is learning how to write
    To write a little book about you!

Fill the Bowl with Rosy Guess What

Wine is the draught
    The poet holds most dear;
He's never quaffed
    The sparkling air like beer.

Milton would groan
    To write about the kin
Of Belial, flown
    With insolence and gin.

Nor Omar to
    The wilderness would hie
With verses, you,
    Bread, and a quart of rye.

Would Jonson ask
    His ladylove to come
And kiss the flask,
    And he'd not ask for rum?

No; wine, wine, wine,
    Is what the poet thinks
The draught divine.
    It's seldom what he drinks.

Thunder on the Left

(On reading in an old issue of "Time" that, in 1953, Stanley L. Miller, under the direction of Harold Urey, had simulated conditions that prevailed on primitive earth, and had created out of its atmospheric gases several organic compounds that are close to proteins)

A horrid planet on its first career
Was Earth. Volcanoes, red and naked-new,
Spouted their belly-gas for atmosphere,
And furious constant thunderbolts shot through

The vapors, making thus amino acid,
Essential (need I say?) to the formation
Of proteins, which are basic to the placid
Process of all organic generation.

—I met a chemist, somewhat eminent;
And he came shouting with unseemly glee:
"I have performed the great experiment
Which Stanley Miller did in '53!

"Water, ammonia, methane, hydrogen
I first prepare, in interesting gas
Such as enwrapped our infant globe, and then
Through it electrical discharges pass—

"A laboratory lightning. I obtain
Glycine, of course, and alpha-alanine
And beta-alanine. I won't explain
The possibilities that supervene,

"But something like Creation has occurred!"
He capered in his bliss. The blazing sky
Was empty. But far off, by Jove, I heard
A fretful thunder. Quick, I said goodbye.

Tuning In with the Infinite

'Twas winter when I won my dear,
  And "Yes!" she whispered low;
And did the sun beam forth to hear,
  And the glad sky gently glow?
    Why, no;
    The skies were dark, in mourning dressed;
    The wind continued west-northwest.

And on our joyful wedding day
  Our hearts were light; but oh,
Did Nature put her threats away,
  Her menaces forgo?
    Why, no;
    Nature was wroth, and all men wondered;
    It rained, hailed, lightened, snowed and thundered.

And now the sun beams radiantly,
  And earth's a wondrous show;
Does Nature in her jealousy
  Prepare a vengeful blow?
    Why, no;
    Emotions don't affect the weather;
    You must be crazy altogether.

Artificial

Oh, his brow was very black,
  And his manner was judicial,
And he said, "Alas! alack!
  Life is now so artificial!

"Lovers once would go to meet
  Death in mighty manly fashion;
We, with artificial heat,
  Sigh our artificial passion;

"Life and food and poetry
  On one formula are founded:
They are artificially
  Colored, flavored, and compounded.

"Now I read, alack! alas!
  News that we may see our doom in;
Some accurst inventor has
  Made an artificial human!"

For the Park I saw him make,
  And he plunged, demanding pardon,
In the artificial lake
  Of the artificial garden.

Some policemen, standing nigh,
  Brought about his extrication,
And restored existence by
  Artificial respiration.

Come, Let Us Muse a Moment on the Pig

Come, let us muse a moment on the pig,
Pitiful pig, whom Man elects to flout,
Sneering and fleering at the shapely snout
Which tells the truffle-hunter where to dig,
Pickling the dainty feet so trim and trig,
Casting him but the meats the diners scout
Which he must eat in shame or go without;
Oh Fate! How hardly whirls your whirligig!

Yet are the mockers mute, the jeerers dumb
In that transfiguring hour when he appears
As Whole Roast Pig, in mouth uplift an apple,
And sausage garlanded about his ears;
"Sweet Swine! O perfect porker!" whisper some.
Yet some there be who love him best as scrapple.

$E = mc^2$

What was our trust, we trust not,
  What was our faith, we doubt;
Whether we must or must not
  We may debate about.
The soul perhaps is a gust of gas
  And wrong is a form of right—
But we know that Energy equals Mass
  By the Square of the Speed of Light.

What we have known, we know not,
  What we have proved, abjure.
Life is a tangled bow-knot,
  But one thing still is sure.
Come, little lad; come, little lass,
  Your docile creed recite:
"We know that Energy equals Mass
  By the Square of the Speed of Light."

The Complete Misanthropist

I love to think of things I hate
    In moments of mopishness;
I hate people who sit up straight,
And youths who smirk about their "date,"
    And the dates who smirk no less.

I hate children who clutch and whine,
    And the arrogant, virtuous poor;
And critical connoisseurs of wine,
And everything that is called a shrine,
    And Art and Literature.

I hate eggs and I hate the hen;
    I hate the rooster, too.
I hate people who wield the pen,
I hate women and I hate men;
    And what's more, I hate you.

To Mr. Mack Sennett, on His Animated Pictures

SENNETT! Regard, I pray, our cinema—
Its endless reels of rancid agonies,
The drear dilemmas of its formula.
There is no laughter in Los Angeles.

CHAPLIN, arouse! Up, up, my HAROLD LLOYD!
Ah, where is CONKLIN? MABEL NORMAND, where?
Only the coils of Technicolored FREUD
Discharge their nonsense on the shuddering air.

Betimes a notice strikes the casual eye:
"You'll scream, you'll yell, you'll whoop at A or B!
You'll foam and froth and faint at X and Y!"
Let others titter. They amuse not me.

Ah, no. I'll bid old memories arise,
Let the dead pan of LANGDON soothe my soul,
Watch TURPIN roll his independent eyes,
And the flung custard seek its human goal.

Thought for Today

(Reproduction prohibited)

> The Preacher spoke of Modern Life,
> In blasting words he blighted it,
> He cursed our economic strife,
> He bombed and dynamited it.
> "My Word," he cried, "will rock the state,
> 'Twill far and wide reverberate;
> The Fancy Feature Syndicate
> Has kindly copyrighted it."
>
> Sin was obliged to toe the line,
> Iniquity was gibbeted;
> He prayed a prayer; it sounded fine
> (Perhaps a bit too glib, it did).
> You'll find his little daily prayer
> Is syndicated here and there—
> But note the "Copyright—Beware!
> Illegal Use Prohibited!"
>
> Of course I know that labor's hire
> The Preacher well could vindicate,
> But certain saints whom I admire
> (Their names I will not indicate)
> Would have regretted much to see
> Their revelation, for a fee,
> "Exclusively the Property
> Of Fancy Feature Syndicate!"

Parfum d'Amour

Sweetest perfumes, sweetest scents
Have a heart of violence;
Fragrances of fairyland
Owe their glamor to the gland
Of the musk-secreting deer.
Even the rose is dry and sere
Till the attar has been treated
With the essence that's secreted
By the loathly civet-cat
In its Afric habitat.
In the lily's no surcease
If it lacks the ambergris
That mysterious fates predestine
In the sickly whale's intestine.
Thus the beauty we adore
Hides a horror at the core.
All of which, my dear, does not
Keep me from exclaiming, "What
Lovely scent delights my nose!
Ah, the lily! Ah, the rose!"

Song of the Pop-Bottlers

Pop bottles pop-bottles
   In pop shops;
The pop-bottles Pop bottles
   Poor Pop drops.

When Pop drops pop-bottles,
   Pop-bottles plop!
Pop-bottle-tops topple!
   Pop mops slop!

Stop! Pop'll drop bottle!
   Stop, Pop, stop!
When Pop bottles pop-bottles,
   Pop-bottles pop!

It's Only Ice-Water

"It's only ice-water. Fill it up,"
You say. You say it's thin as rice-water.
The shaker leans to kiss the cup.
    "It's only ice-water!"

"Truly, it seems to sting," I cry,
    "Sharp as the sting of angry fly-swatter;
But shall I give my host the lie?
    No! It is ice-water!

"Dispute, dissension, make an end!
    War of opinion's worse than price-war!
I will proclaim with you, my friend,
    It's olny ice-warr!"

Thoughts on Endorsing a Junior Driving License

My car, my neighbor's collie feels,
  A bison, bull, or moose is;
He tries to nip the hinder wheels
  And shed its mortal juices.
His race's primitive ideals
  He darkly reproduces.

The motor of my car to me
  Still a vestigial horse is.
With phantom reins instinctively
  I guide him on his courses.
The operation thus we see
  Of old ancestral forces.

My car's a kind of extra limb
  In Junior's estimation.
Between them there exists a dim
  Umbilical relation,
And he is it and it is him
  By consubstantiation.

I gather what the Greeks must mean:
Beware the God from the Machine.

The Electrician's Love Song

Within my heart throughout the past
  Science predominated,
And through magnetic fields it passed
  Completely insulated.

Those bodies charged and dangerous
  That struggled to entwine us
Passed near me registering +
  But I was always −

And then I came within your field;
  'Twas surely providential,
For suddenly I felt revealed
  The force of your potential!

Your power is ruthlessly applied,
  Ever I thrill and quiver,
More positively electrified,
  But you are negativer!

Ever you flee away from me
  As if my love confounded you;
Where is your conductivity?
  Has some disaster grounded you?

The force between us, you're aware—
  You'll pardon my insistence—
Varies inversely as the square
  Of intervening distance.

Who has shortcircuited our arcs?
  Let's banish all deterrents
And turn our intermittent sparks
  To alternating currents!

My voltage is tremendous; oh,
    I would your heart were warmer—
I would I were your dynamo
    And you were my transformer!

Fragment from "The Maladjusted: A Tragedy"

Upon his frustrate and unhopeful quest
  He trod the concrete road of desperation,
And in no Rest Room found he any rest
  Nor was there comfort in a Comfort Station.

He asked for beauty in a Beauty Shop
  In vain; for all their beauty was but shoddy.
So to his life he put a sudden stop.
  The Body Shop would not receive his body.

Psalm of Life
(Greater New York)

Morning. The city's heart dilates
  (To put it somewhat nastily)
And millions it ingurgitates
  In an immense diastole.

Evening contracts the city's heart.
  And men (I see them mistily)
Along unnumbered veins depart
  In a gigantic systole.

A pretty thought. "But how about
  Weekends?" a critic fustily
Objects. The city's heart, no doubt,
  Then merely flutters gustily.

Melody for Lute and Ocarina

Oh, pure is the poppy on the prairie,
  And cheery the chipper chickadee,
And snug is the bug as it snuggles in a rug,
  And solemn the sobbing of the sea;
And lush, love, is mush with molasses,
  And honeyed the proboscis of the bee,
And dear is a steer to the farm overseer,
  But dearer you are to me.

The clergyman cleaves to his cloister,
  The gnat loves to gnaw at the gnu,
At Easter every feaster loves the hoister of the oyster,
  The dewberry drinks in the dew;
The waxwork woos in the wardrobe
  When the waxwork's week's work's through;
The male whale flails the female with his tail,
  But, darling, I love you.

Gas and Hot Air

"Why should not an ingenious and erudite poet take some such preg-
nant subject as architecture, the garden, or the evolution of religion,
or, if he have the knowledge and the boldness, machinery, medicine, or
economics, and dispute Virgil's supremacy in this field, as Virgil once
did Hesiod's?"—R. C. Trevelyan: *Thamyris, or Is There a Future for
Poetry?*

Brooding upon its unexerted power,
   Deep in the gas-tank lay the gasoline
Awaiting the inevitable hour
   When from the inward soul of the machine
Would come the Call. Ah, hark! Man's touch awakes
   Th' ignition switch! The starting-motor hums;
A sound of meshing gears, releasing brakes!
   The call of Duty to the gas-tank comes!

"Vacuum pulls me; and I come! I come!"
   The Gas cried, down the hidden arteries going;
It plashed within the tank of vacuum,
   From th' upper chamber to the lower flowing,
And past the Flapper Valve, which cried, "Ah, stay!
   Stay with the Flapper Valve, the noted petter!"
Heedless, the Gas went grimly on its way
   To fiery nuptials with the carbureter!

Throttled and choked by furious Choke and Throttle,
   By Butterfly valves a-flutter, pet cocks clucking,
Came Gasoline, with gurgling epiglottal
   To the float-chamber, D, the thirsty-sucking;
And to the mixing-chamber came in spray
   Where evermore the gusty air is blowing
And jets of gasoline forever play—
   Of course, provided that the motor's going.

This is the secret bridal chamber where
   The earth-born gas first comes to kiss its bride,

The heaven-born and yet inviolate air
    Which is, on this year's models, purified.
The air, then, enters at the air valve, E,
    The gas is sucked through nozzles from below
(The extra nozzle, J; the normal, C).
    What happens then the picture does not show.

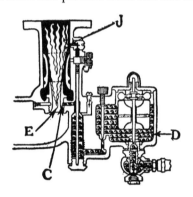

And it is well; for wrapped in close embrace,
    Maddened, they hasten from the bridal room
To that steel-jacketed combustion space
    Where passion bursts against the walls of Doom....
Now frenzy's dead; young frenzy's strength is lost;
    And the exhaust-port gapes for passion's shard;
The ghost of gas wails down the dark exhaust,
    Outworn, burnt out, exhausted—like the bard.

"And We in Dreams Behold the Hebrides"

Divine Nostalgia! Admirable boon,
   Turning the homing heart to yesteryear,
Bringing to dreamer and to stern tycoon
   Alike the blameless and delightful tear!

O blest Emotion! Which in silence conquers
   Outrageous Time! By whose enchanting spell
Old suns shine still on many-peopled Yonkers!
   Taking remembered ways, again I smell

The carpets moldering in a ghostly flat,
   And touch the rubber plant with a curious hand.
Still on the hatrack hangs the quiet hat
   By the umbrella in the umbrella stand.

Public Aid for Niagara Falls

Upon the patch of earth that clings
　　Near the very brink of doom,
Where the frenzied water flings
　　Downward to a misty gloom,

Where the earth in terror quakes
　　And the water leaps in foam
Plunging, frantic, from the Lakes,
　　Hurrying seaward, hurrying home,

Where Man's little voice is vain,
　　And his heart chills in his breast
At the dreadful yell of pain
　　Of the waters seeking rest;

There I stood, and humbly scanned
　　The miracle that sense appalls,
And I watched the tourists stand
　　Spitting in Niagara Falls.

A Tangled Jingle

Chick's employed in checking chicle,
    Dick is dickering in docks,
Nick has knuckled down to nickel,
    Mick makes Michael's Cycle-Socks.

Chick and Dick and Nick and Mick'll
    Chuckle, chortle, chat and chin
At the pretty pickle fickle
    Futile Fate'll fit 'em in.

"For a nickel Nick'll truckle;
    For a shekel Mick'll wreck
Trains, the yokel!" Dick'll chuckle;
    Not a chuckle Chick'll check.

The Passionate Semanticist to His Offspring

Child, do not call your tinny train a choo-choo,
To your own ears be true;
For every passing diesel will refute you—
It does not go "Choo-choo."

And do not call your tricycle a gee-gee.
The term refers, of course,
To animals now unfamiliar; e.g.,
You've never seen a horse.

But I consent to bang-bang-bang and rat-tat,
And in the living room
I shall not issue any caveat at
The most resounding Boom.

I Hear America Singing, Credit Lines[1]

The poets go hippety-hoppety
  To the office to draw their pay;
"Proputty, proputty, proputty—"
  That's what I 'ears 'em say.[2]

And there the office factotum
  Watches o'er every phrase,
And if anyone wants to quote 'em,
  By golly, he pays and pays.[3]

A fellow who writes or edits
  And includes a fragment of song
Had better give proper credits
  Or Ascap will do him wrong.[4]

When you read some novelist's hit, mark
  That no one sings or recites
A line unless Marks or Witmark
  Has ceded the copyrights.

Oh, I think it is frightfully funny
  That our words are restricted thus,
But put them all together they spell *money*,
  A name that means the world to us.[5]

---

[1] All rights reserved, including the right to reproduce anything or portions thereof, by the author and publisher.

[2] By permission of the heirs of Alfred, Lord Tennyson, Aldworth, Blackdown above Haslemere, Surrey, England.

[3] From "The Woman Who Pays," by Will D. Cobb, music by Gus Edwards. By permission of the publishers, Edward B. Marks Music Corporation.

[4] From "Frankie and Johnny," author unknown. A reserve fund has been established to pay eventual claims.

[5] From "Mother," words by Howard Johnson and music by T. Morse. By permission of the publishers, Leo Feist, Inc.

Economics of Mortality

A bankrupt mortician in Tryon
Was forced afar to roam.
It takes a heap o' dyin'
To make a Funeral Home.

Revelation in a Tea-room

The women, clothed in fat and silk
  Delicately destroyed a chicken;
And biscuits, gravy, cream, and milk
  Were irremediably stricken.

And when dessert's satiety
  Succeeded to the candied yams,
A revelation came to me.
  "The weight of these abundant hams,"

I cried, "shall safely hold in thrall
  Society's subversive force,
And to the earth centripetal,
  Shall keep her to her chartered course!"

City Science

New Yorkers seldom know
The moon's phases.
At first quarter, last quarter,
No one gazes.

The tides about their feet
They seldom know:
High tide, low tide,
Ebb and flow.

They do not see the birds
Arriving again:
Redbird, redstart,
Redpoll, wren.

But they know the ecology
Of men alive,
The cluster, cling, clash
Within the hive.

Lines Prompted No Doubt by an Escape-Mechanism

Weary of evaluating basic criteria,
Weary of implementing orientation,
Of visualizing motivational factors wearier,
He bade a vindictive farewell to civilization.

The jungle apes sought he out; and upon them spying,
He gained of the simian language a smattering.
"His gesture is a challenge!" the pleased primates were crying.
"It is indeed a dynamic concept!" he heard them chattering.

Song for Cracked Voices

There once was a man
With a burning desire:
"As soon as I can
I want to retire;
Retirement is what
I want to get on to,
And work I will not,
But do what I want to."

With energy vast,
He labored undaunted
In order at last
To do what he wanted.
But when, after all
His struggles were through,
He couldn't recall
What he wanted to do.

Oh, most of us can't
(And much we regret it)
Still want what we want
When able to get it.
But happy, I grant,
Are the fortunate few
Who do what they want
When they know what to do.

Poet Flays Temptations of City Life

Oh, abominable city!
  Home of Babylonian revels!
Luring lights that know not pity!
  Fascinating female devils!
Fell Temptation is a despot
  And his court assembles there,
In the Wicked City—Yes, but
    Where?

I am proof against Temptation,
  I am clad in shining armor,
I would spurn the fascination
  Of a fair but hellish charmer;
From her wiles I am exempted;
  Still, it's strange as it can be
That no charmer yet has tempted
    Me.

Oh, abominable city!
  Laughing Siren of seduction!
Those unhappy men I pity
  Whom you tempted to destruction;
Your Temptation won them; now they
  Cluster helplessly around it;
—But at times I wonder how they
    Found it.

With Every Regret

For many years the undersigned
Has struggled to improve his mind;
He now is mortified and moved
To find it is not much improved.

His unremitting efforts were
To build a sterling character;
The best that he can really claim
Is that it is about the same.

He went through many a tedious drill
Developing the power of will,
The muscles, and the memory.
They're roughly what they used to be.

Alas! The inference is plain
That Education is in vain,
And all the end of our endeavor
Is to be just as dumb as ever.

Settling Some Old Football Scores

This is the football hero's moment of fame.
Glory is his, though erstwhile he may have shunned it.
In hall and street he hears the crying of his name
    By youth and maiden, alumnus, and radio pundit.

Fierce on the newspaper pages his features show,
    He smites his foe in the innumerable cinema
And in a myriad maidens' dreams. But oh,
    In literature his fame has reached its minima!

See, in the Broadway drama, what he has become, he
    Who was the triply-threatening All-American!
He is a lubberly fellow, a downright dummy!
    And serious fiction is what he is frankly barbaric in.

We read of him telling victories won of yore,
    We see him vainly pursue fame's fleeting bubble;
The maid he adores is certain to leave him for
    A small dark wiry person, the author's double!

O football hero! Now while a million throats
    Acclaim thy glorious deeds, just set this much down;
A small dark wiry person is taking notes.
    Literature will make the ultimate touchdown.

The Ecstasy of Mr. Price

Mr. Price has assumed the fetal position,
   Huddled, snuggled, on the driver's seat.
He touches his little hand to the ignition
   To feel the great, loving motor beat.

In the upholstered womb he has found security,
   He's fled from the world's weary woes away.
O cradling wash of bliss and lost purity!
   Almighty Almotor Mother! O Chevrolet!

Remarks on the Proposed Abandonment
of the Rutland Railroad

Oh, who will save the Rutland,
 That Northern traffic link?
Like ships that sank at Jutland
 We watch the Rutland sink.

Her profits stand at zero,
 Her men she payeth not;
There's sorrow at South Hero
 And woe at Isle La Motte.

And if she cease to function,
 The times are out of joint
North from Hoosick Junction,
 South from Rouses Point.

So Time turns back its pages,
 The Age of Steam is done.
Again the six-horse stages
 Will roll through Bennington;

We'll hear the postboy's banter,
 The coach horn's merry blast,
As through Vermont we canter,
 The country of the past.

And we shall sigh, beholding
 The sumac's fiery spray
And the high weeds enfolding
 The Rutland right of way.

Bible Story

Jael
Hammered a nail
Into the skull of Sisera.
I'd
Rather have tried
A softer spot in the viscera.

"Oh you kid!"
Shouted Id.
"Take it easy, amigo,"
Muttered Ego.

"Babe, we'll take the lid
Off the town!" said Id.
"What will folks say in Oswego?"
Said Ego.

"Babe, let's get rid
Of this killjoy," said Id.
"If I go, will she go?"
Said Ego.

Vast and calm and politic
Super-Ego swung his stick.
Super-Ego turned his head:
"You boys better get back to bed."
"Well, I never did!"
Said Id.

I Mused by Ritz's Bowery Rill

Five little ducklings
　Swimming at the Ritz,
Heedless of the chucklings
　Of the exquisites;

Fat little lumpkins
　In the Ritz pond,
Waggling their rumpkins
　Before the beau monde!

World-famous beauties
　Gurgle with glee:
"Such little cuties!
　Qu'ils sont gentils!"

But change is incessant;
　The ducks on the mere
Become adolescent
　And then disappear.

The headwaiter, truckling
　Before the gourmet,
Urges roast duckling—
　Spécialité.

Ah, *lex est perire,*
　The poet admits.
The dictum so dreary
　Applies to the Ritz.

The Freedom of the Press

I remember when I was a boy
The books that I used to enjoy
Were as likely as not to employ
    A phrase I remember as queer.
For instance: "Then Chimmie the Rat
Turned on his captor and spat
A stream of profanity that
    Is unprintable here."

Or: "The buses collided, and both
Drivers emitted an oath
Unprintable!" or, perhaps, "Quoth
    The mule-skinner, urging his mules:
'Giddap, you unprintable jacks!
Or I'll land some unprintable whacks
Upon your unprintable backs,
    You unprintable fools!' "

I think we may fairly conclude
That blasphemous language and lewd
Would over and over intrude
    In the idiom spoken by men.
And I think my examples will teach
That as far as our memories reach
The speakable phrases of speech
    Were unprintable then.

But custom has changed with a rush;
I open a book and I blush:
I close it again, crying "Hush!"
    No reading aloud I allow.
I halt, when I see with dismay
The words that I never could say.
The printable words of today
    Are unspeakable now.

The Voice from the Privet Hedge

As sweet Mrs. Pugh down the sidewalk was faring
    And no living creature appeared to her view,
The privet hedge spoke with a terrible blaring,
    "Repent of your sins, Mrs. Pugh!"

The practical joker, John Anthony Trivett,
    Leaned out of his window and gave a halloo.
He'd had a loudspeaker installed in the privet
    To terrify sweet Mrs. Pugh.

She covered her panic with ladylike ruses,
    And brightly she grinned in response to his grins.
How strange are the instruments Providence chooses!
    Mrs. Pugh *did* repent of her sins.

The Happy Solipsist

Sol'ip-sism. *Philos.* The theory or belief that only knowledge of the self is possible and therefore that for each individual mind itself is the only thing really existent.

How happy is the solipsist,
  Who looks abroad and does not find
That either you or I exist
  Except as figments of his mind!

For him the woes of earth subside,
  He sees them all with humorous phlegm;
And all its beauties are his pride,
  For he has just created them.

I met a taxi-driver once
  Who put his faith in solipsism;
For him the world and its affronts
  Were products of his organism,

And I, his passenger, the least
  And last of his phenomena,
Whose fearful outcries but increased
  His glad, omnipotent huzza.

To Lands of Wonder

The little girl and little boy
Of long ago in ancient Greece
Were often able to enjoy
The story of the Golden Fleece
Sung by a strolling bard. Or else
A Phrygian hostler in the stables,
While currying the horses' pelts
Would tell them one of Aesop's fables.
But oh! their case was sad indeed!
They had no children's books to read.

The little girl and little boy
On rainy days in ancient Rome
Would hear the woeful lay of Troy
And how Aeneas fled his home.
They knew the memorable fate
Of Remus and of Romulus;
They'd hear an Ethiop slave relate
Tales of the hippopotamus.
But never a Roman undertook
To give a child a children's book!

Now children steal away to meet
The fairies in a magic wood;
They talk with beasts in their retreat
And draw the bow with Robin Hood.
Quiet; do not disturb the dream
That for a moment has beguiled
Into a land where wonders gleam
The beautiful enchanted child
Hidden within his holy nook,
Alone, reading a children's book.

Happy Ending

I used to laugh at folly,
    At men's absurdities;
I found extremely jolly
    Idiosyncrasies
Of people wooing money
    Or following a fad—
These used to strike me funny;
    Now they strike me sad.

The trickeries of vandals,
    Society's pretense,
And governmental scandals,
    And office-insolence,
Vagaries economic,
    Athletic, dietetic—
I used to find them comic;
    Now they seem pathetic.

And yet, the large abstractions,
    Eternities and Fates,
Mortality's exactions,
    The issue that awaits
The gloomy and the glad,
    The sorry and the sunny—
They used to strike me sad;
    Now they strike me funny.

LIMERICKS

When a feverish groom in Amenia
Had nibbled away his gardenia,
   They just let him graze
   On the bridesmaids' bouquets,
To quiet the old neurasthenia.

A strong-minded lady of Arden
Grows nothing but burrs in her garden;
  She tosses the burrs
  On passing chauffeurs,
And never begs anyone's pardon.

There's a tiresome young man in Bay Shore;
When his fiancée cried, "I adore
　　The beautiful sea!"
　　He replied, "I agree
It's pretty; but what is it for?"

The people of Candlewood Knolls
Are terribly troubled by trolls,
  Who are driving their cars,
  And brawling in bars,
And voting for Thor at the polls.

For a patron of Carnegie Hall
The ushers remain within call;
  When a certain motif
  Makes him shake like a leaf,
They tie up his head in a shawl.

There's a whimsical fellow in Deal
Who barks for his food like a seal;
  Says his wife, with a sniff:
  " 'Twould be funnier, if
He'd skip an occasional meal!"

A clergyman startled Dobbs Ferry
By rubbing his bald head with sherry;
  As his hostess looked pained,
  He humbly explained:
"They say it prevents beri-beri."

A clergyman out in Dumont
Keeps tropical fish in the font;
   Though it always surprises
   The babes he baptizes,
It seems to be just what they want.

A youth who afflicts Essex Fells
Can yell University yells,
   From Abilene's hail
   To the frog-call of Yale;
He also puts poison in wells.

Said old Peeping Tom of Fort Lee:
"Peeping ain't what it's cracked up to be;
   I lose all my sleep,
    And I peep and I peep,
And I find 'em all peeping at me."

Said a fervent young lady of Hammels,
"I object to humanity's trammels!
   I want to be free!
   Like a bird! Like a bee!
Oh, why am I classed with the mammals?"

There's a vaporish maiden in Harrison
Who longed for the love of a Saracen.
   But she had to confine her
   Intent to a Shriner,
Who suffers, I fear, by comparison.

A ghoulish old fellow in Kent
Encrusted his wife in cement;
   He said, with a sneer:
   "I was careful, my dear,
To follow your natural bent."

An inventive young man in Monroe
Built a weather-conditioned château;
  By his technical blunders
  The dining-room thunders,
And the bathrooms incessantly snow.

"I have heard," said a maid of Montclair,
"Opportunity's step on the stair;
  But I couldn't unlock
  To its magical knock,
For I always was washing my hair."

A joker who haunts Monticello
Is really a terrible fellow;
   In the midst of caresses
   He fills ladies' dresses
With garter-snakes, ice-cubes, and jell-o.

A philosopher out in Mount Holly
Writes books on the world and its folly;
   When he has to relax
   From his savage attacks,
He likes to play train with his dolly.

A pushing young man in Patchogue
Runs a Radio Hour for the Dog.
  His program of growls,
  Barks, bays, whines, and howls
Is setting the dog world agog.

There was a young fellow of Pelham
Who caught the Dutch blight from an ellum;
   "It's a bore," were his words,
   "On account of the birds,
For I have to get sprayed to dispel 'em."

There's a lady in Pocono Pines
Who hides in historical shrines,
  And emerges from beds
  Of our national heads
To leer at the visitors' lines.

At spirit-séances in Queens
The spirits make terrible scenes;
   Thus recently Bach
   Shouted angrily: "Ach!
I'm sick of your damn tambourines!"

A modernist preacher of Redding
Pioneered with a Parachute Wedding;
  But the bride's wedding-gown
  Just wouldn't stay down;
And you can't keep a cassock from spreading.

A naturalist in Roselle
Has developed a keen sense of smell;
  Blindfolded, his game is
  To tell what your name is.
But still, after all, what the hell?

A contemptuous lady in Shoreham
Behaved with extreme indecorum;
   She snapped a sarcastic
   And secret elastic
Throughout the Community Forum.

There's a dowager near Sneden Landing
Whose manners are bluff and commanding;
   It is one of her jests
   To trip up her guests,
For she hates to keep gentlemen standing.

There's a sensitive type in Tom's River
Whom Beethoven causes to quiver;
  The esthetic vibration
  Brings soulful elation,
And also is fine for the liver.

For years an old mother in Troy
Sobbed: "Where is my wandering boy?"
  Till they said: "Why not look
  In the telephone book?"
And she dialled his number with joy.

A credulous lady of Utica'll
Believe any ad pharmaceutical,
   Though a little unmanned
   By removing her hand,
When she planned on removing her cuticle.

A one-day-old baby in Wallabout
Reflected: "Oh, what is it all about?
  I comprehend not
  Whence, whither, or what,
But I'm sure it is something to squall about."

MUSEUM THOUGHTS

Sweet Allegory! Thus does Genius rise,
Propp'd by Imagination, to the skies!
Thus does the Poet try his new-fledg'd talents,
Learning on perilous perch to keep his balance.

But Allegory need not be confin'd
To the sole operations of the mind.
Thus, in the tumid nursling we may see
Some eager-gaping Infant Industry
Incorporate at governmental font,
Mother'd by Law and father'd by du Pont.
His quiv'ring, dewy pinions are unfurl'd
To all the gusts of th' economic world.

O Babe! Thou mayest represent, in fact,
Equally well the North Atlantic Pact,
Or Noise Abatement, or the New Japan,
Or some Prefabricated-Housing Plan.

For Allegory fits with any story;
Perchance it here betokens Allegory.

I said, bewildered, to the Missis,
"I don't get what this Nemesis is."
The Missis said, a trifle gloomy,
"I clearly see what's coming to me.
I clearly see that Albrecht Dürer
Reveals how ladies get maturer.
The artist here depicts with vigor
The Nemesis of woman's figure.
'Gird up your loins!' Oh, surely this is
The helpful hint of Nemesis's."

Everybody likes to go
To the artist's studio.
Oh what frolic, oh what fun!
Bring your monkey, deer, and gun,
Bring your dog along, of course,
And by all means bring your horse.
We will box and we will fence,
Practise playing instruments;
Always there's a jolly show
In the artist's studio.

Who's the member of the band
At the easel, brush in hand,
Where the trumpet and the drum
Raise a pandemonium?
Who is he, so much engrossed?
Stap my vitals, that's the host,
With remarkable restraint
    Trying to paint.

"Cupid's Despair," by E. Daelen

Why is Cupid sobbing so?
What has happened to his bow?

Cupid spied Corinna maying,
    And maliciously he laughed,
And, his marksmanship displaying,
    He discharged a ribboned shaft,
And the dainty, deadly dart
Lodged in poor Corinna's heart.

And Corinna fell to grieving
    On the daisy-dappled lea,
And I saw her bosom heaving
    As she raptly gazed at me.
Cupid took another dart,
And he aimed it at my heart.

Why is Cupid sobbing so?
Because I bust his goddam bow.

See the Bard—I call him Whozis—
Being courted by the Muses!
Culture's fair ambassadresses
Overwhelm him with caresses,
While a helpful lady fusses
With a quill of Pegasus's.

Poets—also poetesses—
Have you tasted such successes?
Never! It's the bard who chases
Muses, seeking their embraces.

I'm inclined to think the case is
That the title has no basis,
And the proper theme, my guess is,
Is "A Band of Poetesses;"
And the gentleman who poses,
Being crowned with wreaths and roses,
And whom every lady woos, is
Just a publisher named Whozis.

The critics do not much enjoy
Sir Edwin Landseer's "Naughty Boy."
They seem to think it very frightful,
But mothers find it quite delightful.
Why do the critic and the mother
Thus disagree with one another?
No doubt the psychoanalytics
Say naughty boys turn into critics,
For they recall the mother's sanctum
Wherein repeatedly she spanked 'em
And they inhibited their rancor
Against the spanking and the spanker
And compensate by spanking others.
Perhaps more critics should be mothers.

Rubens' "La Petite Pelisse" (A Portrait of His Second Wife, Hélène Fourment)

People say that artists' wives
Lead such interesting lives,
Paying almost no attention
To the dictates of convention,
Always ready for a party,
Wearing clothes bizarre and arty.
Nonetheless, they sometimes think
Longingly of coats of mink.

Rubens' wife (née Helen Fourment)
Once announced, "*Je suis en tourment;*
I am sick of looking shoddy,
Looking worse than anybody.
Peter, are you quite unable
To provide a mink or sable?"
P. P. Rubens said to her,
"I will buy a coat of fur
Of the very finest pelts—
But *absolutely nothing else!*"

Helen Fourment clearly thinks
Useless are the finest minks,
Since her husband, Peter Paul,
Bought her nothing else at all,
Since her wardrobe is so bare
That she hasn't underwear.

Evidently artists' wives
Do lead interesting lives.

Library of Congress Cataloging in Publication Data

BISHOP, MORRIS, 1893–1973.
    The best of Bishop.

        I. Reppert, Charlotte Putnam.   II. New Yorker.
III. Title.
PS3503.I796A6   1980   811'.52   80-66902
ISBN 0-8014-1310-9